"*The Hero and the Whore* is a liberation theolog[ ] the weighty systems of oppression that bear a[ ] era of white Christian nationalism. Camille Hernandez lets us into the moments in her life when her keenly honed critical consciousness comes face-to-face with the supremacist ideologies of white evangelicalism in the United States. She graciously offers us the acts of resistance that have allowed her to engage with biblical texts that have so often been used to support patriarchy and white supremacy. Her readings of Scripture are intuitive and welcoming, inviting the reader to explore how their own story finds meaning within these texts. For anyone feeling pushed to the margins of Christianity, *The Hero and the Whore* is an excellent spiritual guide for determining what is worthwhile investment in our well-being and what needs to be left behind."
—**Sara Moslener**, author of *Virgin Nation*

"In a time when many are at a crossroads and experiencing deep crises of faith, a necessary theological voice has emerged. What Hernandez has done in the pages of this book will heal us now, help heal the wounds of the past, and work to heal generations to come. We have needed her and this amazing offering, and I'm so glad they are both here!"
—**Candice Marie Benbow**, author of *Red Lip Theology*

"If you're looking for a book that blends tender care, moving poetry, and careful biblical scholarship, you need to read *The Hero and the Whore*. Hernandez leads us through the realities of oppression and liberation, reminding us that we don't have to stay in the toxic colonial spaces that many of us are born into and that we can bravely wrestle with questions we don't always have answers for. As you enter deeper into the words and poetry found in these pages, you'll experience the passion of an abolitionist and the hands of a caretaker as Hernandez leads us into stories of trauma, colonization, and oppression and through them to the other side. In the time in which we are living, we need books that help us tell the truth and help us dream, and this book is one of them."
—**Kaitlin B. Curtice**, award-winning author
of *Native and Living Resistance*

"Those of us steeped in white, patriarchal ways of theology and biblical interpretation have been given an incomplete gospel; we swim on the surface of a deep ocean of truth and beauty that we often do not know how to experience. Camille Hernandez helps us to see women in Scripture in ways our own social locations often make us blind to and, in the process, equips us to be partners in the liberation God desires for us all. This book will stretch your heart and mind in all the ways we need to be stretched."

—**Chris Furr**, author of *Straight White Male*

"By centering the oft-silenced women of the Scriptures, Hernandez shows us that these living stories can lead to liberation. In *The Hero and the Whore*, the marginalized voices of the Bible beckon readers beyond the limiting expectations of broken societies to a more universal thriving where all are free to be whom they were created to be."

—**Trey Ferguson**, pastor, writer, and podcaster

"Reading Hernandez is like sitting next to a well filled with the tears of every woman who has felt the pain of violence, silence, and invisibility. *The Hero and the Whore* offers liberatory stories that reclaim the voices of women in society and the Bible that have been stifled by patriarchy and power. If you're ready to read stories from a perspective that brings awareness to violence, read this book and let it transform your understanding."

—**Terence Lester**, founder of Love beyond Walls and author of *All God's Children, I See You*, and *When We Stand*

"Hernandez's words will infuse those in need of healing and liberation with the courage to seek and claim them as their rightful inheritance. She is the perfect person to have by our side as we birth new narratives of our inherent worth and beauty, no matter what our stories have been up to this point. This book oozes with brilliance and love."

—**Marla Taviano**, author of *unbelieve* and *jaded*

"In a day that has popularized 'deconstruction,' Hernandez's lovingly and thoughtfully crafted book is a dive into a spirituality that is full of questions, wonder, and bravery. The way that she explicitly names harmful ideologies *and* ways of repair has left me hopeful about what my faith can be."

—**Robert Monson**, codirector of Enfleshed.com

The Hero and the Whore

The Hero and the Whore

Reclaiming Healing and Liberation through Stories of Sexual Exploitation in the Bible

CAMILLE HERNANDEZ

WESTMINSTER
JOHN KNOX PRESS
LOUISVILLE • KENTUCKY

© 2023 Camille Hernandez
Foreword © 2023 Westminster John Knox Press

First edition
Published by Westminster John Knox Press
Louisville, Kentucky

Published in association with The Bindery Agency, www.TheBinderyAgency.com.

23 24 25 26 27 28 29 30 31 32—10 9 8 7 6 5 4 3 2 1

All rights reserved. No part of this book may be reproduced or transmitted in any form or by any means, electronic or mechanical, including photocopying, recording, or by any information storage or retrieval system, without permission in writing from the publisher. For information, address Westminster John Knox Press, 100 Witherspoon Street, Louisville, Kentucky 40202-1396. Or contact us online at www.wjkbooks.com.

Unless otherwise indicated, Scripture quotations are from the New Revised Standard Version, Updated Edition, copyright © 2021 National Council of Churches of Christ in the United States of America. Used by permission. All rights reserved worldwide. Scripture quotations marked MSG are taken from *The Message*, copyright © 1993, 2002, 2018 by Eugene H. Peterson. Used by permission of NavPress. All rights reserved. Represented by Tyndale House Publishers, Inc.

Book design by Sharon Adams
Cover design by Mary Ann Smith

Library of Congress Cataloging-in-Publication Data is on file at the Library of Congress, Washington, DC.

ISBN-13: 978-0-664-26821-3

Most Westminster John Knox Press books are available at special quantity discounts when purchased in bulk by corporations, organizations, and special-interest groups. For more information, please e-mail SpecialSales@wjkbooks.com.

Contents

Author's Note

These stories and topics are triggering. Please take whatever breaks you need as you read this book. I believe that for us to heal, it's important to name violence and acknowledge the harm it has caused. I also believe in taking breaks and having boundaries. I invite you to exercise both as you read.

This book is not a mental health guide or a step-by-step manual for healing from trauma. I highly recommend seeking out a culturally competent mental health specialist—therapist, counselor, or social worker—as well as a community of folks with whom to have gentle and honest conversations.

Land Back Statement

This book was written on occupied land of the Gabrielino-Tongva, Kizh, and Acjechemen nations, whose people stewarded the lands currently known as Los Angeles, Orange, and San Diego counties. They are still alive today despite unfair laws, enslavement, pandemic, and genocide. They have known this land for 10,000 years.

Both nations were enslaved by Spanish conquistadors and forced into providing the physical labor necessary to build the California missions. The Gabrielino-Tongva and Kizh peoples were enslaved to build the San Gabriel Mission in the City of San Gabriel and the San Fernando Mission in the City of Los Angeles. The Acjechemen tribe was forced by enslavement to build the San Juan Capistrano Mission of Orange County.

Before the Spanish conquistadors came and violently forced their religion and unethical standards onto these peoples, the Gabrielino-Tongva, Kizh, and Acjechemen nations thrived as stewards of the land who worked in tandem with nature to cultivate equitable systems of care and provision for their peoples.

This book was written with the spirit of Toypurina in mind. She was a Kizh medicine woman who recruited other Indigenous peoples to revolt against the Spanish conquistadors at the San Gabriel Mission. She and her coconspirators were captured and imprisoned. During her trial, Toypurina famously said, "I hate the padres and all of you, for living here on my native soil, . . . for trespassing on the land of my forefathers and despoiling our tribal domains." After imprisonment she was forcibly baptized into Christianity and forced into exile from her people.

The Hero and the Whore is written to recognize the many ways Western Christianity has conducted sexual violence against marginalized peoples as a tool in perpetrating forms of oppression including, but not limited to, colonialism, enslavement, genocide, and ecoterrorism. First we acknowledge the land that was invaded, the Indigenous peoples who were attacked, and—most importantly—we recognize the generations of Indigenous resistance done to restore the peoples and the lands.

For true healing and reconciliation to occur, and in order to reverse the harmful effects of Christian colonialism's violence against women, trans and gender-expansive people, and against the land, we must work to ensure that the land is restored to its original stewards and that Indigenous land sovereignty is centered within our movement for liberation. Give the land back.

Foreword

"I never wanted to be an ethicist." Those were the words that Katie Geneva Cannon uttered to a shocked audience at the Samuel Dewitt Proctor Conference in February 2018, just six months before her death from acute leukemia, as she accepted the Beautiful Are Their Feet award. Cannon went on to say that the Old Testament had always been her passion. But when she began her doctoral work at Union Theological Seminary, she was told that she could not concentrate in Old Testament because the school did not want to be the first institution to allow a Black woman to enroll in what was considered an elite field "traditionally reserved for the white men with the most powerful political connections."[1] Cannon instead became the first Black woman to earn a PhD in ethics and, upon the publication of *Katie's Canon* in 1988, one of the founders of womanist theology. Women like Katie Cannon, Jacquelyn Grant, Delores Williams, Kelly Brown Douglas, Clarice Martin, Renita Weems, and Emilie Townes created a space for Black women when the Christian theological academy proclaimed that there was "no room at the inn."

With *The Hero and the Whore*, Camille Hernandez makes a space of her own as a kapwa womanist, standing in the legacy of four decades of Black women's ministry and theological scholarship, as well as in her identity as a Filipina and an African American. Like the womanists and Asian American feminists upon whose shoulders she stands, Camille doesn't just create space for herself. She fills a room with

comfy cushions and sofas and invites others to join her. She wrestles
with what Phyllis Trible deemed "texts of terror," biblical passages
in which women are victims of violence, rejection, and exclusion.
These are the texts that make thinking Christians cringe. Where is
the good news in a faith that repeatedly scapegoats women as evil
temptresses or pits them against each other in a struggle for patriarchal attention? What liberation can women—especially women of
color, same-gender-loving, nonbinary, and trans women—find in a
religion whose sacred text exploits our pain as a divine object lesson?
How can we see ourselves as created in the image of God when the
biblical writers often render us nameless, faceless, and invisible? How
can God be on the side of the poor and oppressed when the people
of God use sacred text to justify our oppression and marginalization?

There are no easy answers to these questions. Fortunately, Camille
does not try to offer any. Instead, she draws upon her experience and
perspective as a trauma-informed caregiver to disrupt the narrative
that salvation is to be found in Western imperialist Christianities that
extol violence, conquest, genocide, and rape. She helps us to confront and resist the lies and silences that keep us bound to hetero-
sexist White supremacist Christian nationalism. Where mainstream
Christianity (including evangelicals, mainline Protestants, and the
historical Black church traditions) offers weak apologetics for these
stories or simply turns its head away, Camille approaches them much
like Jacob did the angel at the Jabbok River in Genesis 32, wrestling
a blessing (or something like it) out of them. She reframes the stories
of the "bad girls of the Bible" using an explicitly womanist lens. She
is not content to simply accept these stories at face value. She exercises a prophetic imagination to frame each of these women against
the harshly patriarchal contexts that constrained their choices for
survival.

Camille likely does not identify as either a biblical scholar or a
theologian, but here she is both, and in the best sense. This is decon-
structivism, to be sure, but it is also constructive, practical, and deeply
personal. Through her eyes we get to see each of these women as
people we know, perhaps even people we are, have been, or could be.
We see the direct connection between the struggles of their lives and
those of our own time, including purity and rape culture, assimilation

and cultural erasure, conquest and genocide, racism, sexuality, and gender identity. And prayerfully, as we see each of their narratives remade, we find ways to remake our relationship with Scripture. We learn some new wrestling techniques.

When Katie Cannon realized that the church and the academy lacked the liberating lens that she needed, she decided to make it herself. And she repeatedly enjoined Black women to "do the work your soul must have." Camille has done the work that many a soul needs.

Chanequa Walker-Barnes, PhD

Prologue

Please don't quote John 3:16. . . . Oh no, no no nooooo. . . . Please don't cry.
I was shifting in my seat and mentally pleading with this middle-aged white man to stop crying and to stop quoting Scripture. It was the fifth hour of a daylong missionary training led by a conservative white evangelical organization headed by a bunch of white men. I was tired of sitting in this conference room, tired of the uncomfortable chairs surrounding circular tables, and *definitely* tired of small talk.

The CEO was giving his final thoughts. They were meager, uninspired, and filled with that not-so-subtle cadence that is commonly demonstrated by white evangelical males who want you to *feel* the urgency of God's movement. Just as he finished his final word, another organization leader echoed the sentiment with *the* key Scripture: "For God [sniffle] so loved [sniffle] the world that he [tears, voice cracking] gave his only Son [more tears, and incoherent blubbering that I assume ended the verse]."

Here I was—a Black and Filipina woman sitting next to my Chicano husband—drowning in a sea of whiteness. It was the end of 2016, Philando Castile and Alton Sterling had been murdered by the police, Donald J. Trump had been elected president of the United States, and there were talks of a nationwide women's march that would be happening to protest his election. During this white evangelical training, people openly shared their opinions,

1

and every opinion was anti-Black, misogynist, pro–police brutality, Christian nationalist, and was curated by the ever-inflamed politically conservative white Christian nationalist media. Exacerbating their awful opinions was their inability to act right. One of the men sitting at our table felt moved to convince me that Black liberation theology was demonic. Another person at the table must have been playing microaggression bingo, given how he commented on my hair and skin tone, told me that I don't "look" Asian, and talked of how he was so surprised that I could know so much. As I gave my opinions and retorts, their heads conveniently turned away. It was unfathomable to them that I—a Black and Filipina person—could have a critical thought worth contributing to their dehydrated conversations.

To say that this was the Sunken Place would have been a compliment.

At that time, I was a baby Christian, desperate to give my life to Jesus. I thrust myself into the world of evangelicalism, which used its covert respectability politics to comment on how I was too Black, too Asian, too female, too liberal, and—frankly—too *much* to be anything more than the token outlier needing to constantly be made anew. I thoroughly believed that if I wanted to serve Christ, I had to accept their standards. I convinced myself that the place of violence was the only flourishing place available to me.

In their world, I contained too many demonic identities. To be Black was bad, but to be a Black woman was damaging. To be an Asian woman who spoke freely and interrupted conversation was simply the work of the devil. In order to know the gospel, I had to be loyal to white evangelicalism and Christian nationalism. I did that for nearly a decade. I learned to deny myself, my parentage, my cultures, my ancestry, my intelligence, and my sexuality, and I severed my nonevangelical relationships.

In those years, I learned that violence was holiness.

Violence and Oppression

Before I get to the heart of this book on violence, it's important that I establish a framework for understanding violence and oppression.

We do not live in a world that has concrete definitions of either, and thus these words are thrown around and misappropriated at will and used to create inflammatory accusations. Oppression and violence are synchronous but not synonymous. This means that we cannot switch one term for the other. We need to understand them individually in order to develop our own language and expand our understanding.

Oppression is used to maintain hierarchies among social groups in order to perpetuate a culture that normalizes dominance and subjugation. When speaking of oppression, I refer to Iris Marion Young's article that divides oppression into five categories: exploitation, marginalization, powerlessness, cultural imperialism, and violence.[1]

Exploitation is a system of domination that occurs when a person's labor, skill, and body are forcibly used, without payment, to benefit the entity in power. The benefit includes (but is not specific to) gaining wealth, sexual satisfaction, and higher social standing, and establishing social hierarchies. *Marginalization* occurs when people are categorized according to markers of identity (gender, race, class, age, ability, etc.) in order to expel people, exploit their labor, or exalt the justifications for maintaining systems of power. *Powerlessness*, as Young explains, "describes the lives of people who have little or no work autonomy, exercise little creativity or judgment in their work, have no technical expertise or authority, express themselves awkwardly, especially in public or bureaucratic settings, and do not command respect."[2] *Cultural imperialism* is a strategy that seeks to belittle the voices and experiences of marginalized peoples seeking liberation through use of stereotypes, cultural appropriation, and erasure. The goal of cultural imperialism is to normalize the culture of those in power and deem the other groups as inferior.

The final category, *violence*, extends beyond the definitions that are normative in our cultures. A common misconception of violence is that it is only defined by a physical attack. When I speak of violence, I use the definition that comes from the United Nations Entity for Gender Equality and the Empowerment of Women (also known as UN Women). It lays out a detailed list of the types of violence that impact women and girls. Because this book focuses on the experiences of sexual violence within the Bible, I'm going to explain the differences between domestic violence and sexual violence per UN Women's definitions.

Domestic violence is a form of relational abuse in which one partner seeks to establish dominance over another. Domestic violence includes economic, psychological, emotional, physical, and sexual violence. *Economic violence* includes the ways someone will force financial dependence upon a relationship partner. This includes, but is not limited to, withholding money, controlling financial resources, and forcing or forbidding attendance at work and/or school. *Psychological violence* involves manipulative actions taken to intimidate or coerce others into thinking they must be dependent on their abusers in order to survive. *Emotional violence* is done through making people believe they have little to no self-worth through verbal abuse, gaslighting, damaging outside relationships, and denying opportunities to see friends and family. *Physical violence* includes physical attacks (hitting, punching, pinching, shoving, kicking, etc.), refusal of medical treatment, physical force, and property damage.

Sexual violence is another form of domestic violence, but it has its own subcategories that include sexual harassment, rape, corrective rape, and rape culture.

Sexual harassment is when sexual contact (be it physical or verbal) is done without consent or by way of manipulation. Physical sexual harassment can look like touching, rubbing, grabbing, pinching, and slapping. Verbal sexual harassment includes catcalls, comments on body appearance, demands for sexual favors, and exposing sexual organs. *Rape* is forced sexual penetration (vaginal, anal, oral) with a body part or an object. Rape happens when consent is forcibly revoked and can happen in intimate partner relationships, or from family members, friends, or complete strangers. *Corrective rape* is a form of rape meant to force a heteronormative sexual lifestyle on a person who identifies as lesbian, gay, bisexual, transgender, queer, questioning, intersex, asexual, or agender. *Rape culture* is a patriarchy-rooted form of control in which sexual violence is normalized, justified, and upheld in order to further perpetuate gender inequality. While rape culture is a universal experience, it is particularly violent in how it upholds systems of racism, homophobia, and transphobia.[3]

Frictionless Gospel

My experience in the daylong ministry training hit several nodes on the list of violence and oppression. At that point in my life, I truly believed this was the only way to be a Christian. I dangled on their words and wholeheartedly pursued their white, suburban, individualist, status quo Christ. I told myself that the middle-aged white man who wept as he quoted John 3:16 did so because he could *feel* the urgency of this movement to colonize—ahem, "minister to"—these "unreached peoples." The grandeur of eternal salvation for these low-income communities of color depended solely on the actions of the white evangelical middle-class church and their white Christian nationalist standards.

I fell for Christian urgency, which is used as the blueprint for spreading the gospel. The leader appeals to the collective ethos with a "poor them" narrative, then presents his solution (firmly planted in the white male delusion of grandeur) as the only way for goodness to be done. The message is then neatly wrapped in the pretty bow that is the eschatological promise of eternal life and Instagrammable moments: "These people are poor, but they can have *eternal salvation* through Jesus! Those people could die any moment, but if they receive *our Christ* they'll live forever." Christian urgency is more about controlling the masses than it is about extending care; the only cure to the hellscape was the irony of "freedom in Christ" under their control.

I was trained to give the ultimatum: disciple people in this "very effective" mission strategy, or fail at effectively communicating an understanding of God's love. But according to this logic, God's love was tempered and always in short supply. Godliness, to the leaders of the ministry training, was about upholding the standards of whiteness and maleness. I had no chance of achieving those standards, so God's vast and unending love became a constant critique that paved the way for deep self-loathing.

They spoke of love but were mute about injustice. It was as if words like *genocide*, *slavery*, and *assault* didn't exist in their vocabulary. Bringing them up rendered a Jesus juke and a threat to no longer belong in their little Christian club.

What do you do when leaders can express deep and heartfelt emotions about God but are unable to recognize or acknowledge their own complicity in systems that continually harm people? The God they speak of becomes just as abusive as the ambassadors. When people are unable to publicly acknowledge their role in perpetuating harm, the God they represent is no longer the figure of forgiveness and compassion. They'll spend all that time in the pulpit shouting the name of the Lord and letting the devil live in their actions.

There's a second problem with Christian urgency: it makes salvation a spiritual transaction with only one way to purchase Christ. Say the magic words, or write them on your stuff, and your destiny is secure.

The "cool Christians" in my high school loved to point out how John 3:16 appeared in not-so-secret places: In-N-Out cups, Forever 21 bags, Jesus fish bumper stickers, and Not of This World products. When we saw this verse we'd say, "Isn't it so cool that they're Christian? Look at how they're spreading the gospel." The John 3:16 stamp was meant to set companies apart. Instead, it made this so-called defining verse of Jesus' ministry just as transactional as the purchased items they carried. The gospel—the story of the embodied God who chose to befriend and live among the poor, oppressed, and marginalized—was mass-manufactured and used as advertising content. The vast wonder of the gospel is narrowed down to the transaction. All the other inflections, subtleties, actions, and affections of Jesus are lost. Salvation is purchased through a Bible verse much like the tap of instant pay from a smart watch. There is no longer room for the expanse of humanity; there is only room to revel in the transaction and ensure that it is done correctly.

Frictionless spending garners an exponentially higher profit because it allows the shopper to have a seamless shopping experience with just a swipe, tap, or insert of the card. It's driven on data and minimized human interaction. In return, the seller's profit is maximized with less effort and less need for human connection. Western Christianity assumes the same strategy works in our discipleship. All violence is justified, and our ability to humanize victims is disregarded. The goal is to move the gospel forward by any means necessary.

This is the frictionless gospel: buy salvation, sell Jesus, silence the harm done.

Sexual assault, rape, incest, pedophilia, enslavement, colonization, homophobia—all are tools used to circulate the gospel. Accountability stops being a spiritual practice and becomes a barrier that needs to be destroyed.

In case you were wondering, my husband and I did not end up working for that organization. Maybe it was God navigating our steps. That's a sweet way to put it. I'm pretty sure it was because I told one of the directors that their proposed ministry model sounded like colonization.

Oopsies.

Prophetic Disruption

From 2016 to 2021 my husband and I "worked" in pastoral ministry with people who have experienced high levels of trauma. I use quotes around the word *worked* because that term implies that we clocked in and out. We used some of the transactional strategies we gained from that awful training; at the same time we were being trained in the model of trauma-informed care by a separate organization. As ministers we came across constant challenges where we had to question which model worked in each specific situation. Sometimes we chose well, and other times we unknowingly sowed discord. Who would trust the ministry of a person who has been trained to hate themselves and unknowingly spread that hate to others?

During those years we lived our lives according to Eugene Peterson's poetic translation: "The Word became flesh and blood, and moved into the neighborhood" (John 1:14 MSG). Instead, we *lived*. We lived with people accustomed to violence because we too were people who grew up accustomed to violence. There was not much difference between us and our neighbors. We raised our children together. We laughed, cried, and found ourselves exposed and lacking. Our paper-thin walls knew the words that a parent would scream at their child and the hushed sobs of an abused spouse. Our senses became attuned to the signs of domestic violence, and our bodies knew stillness when confronted with unbridled rage. Our home was the prayer closet, and our windows became the portal of evidence of why the hope of Christ was needed. We realized that all the training we received on being an "effective missionary" was like Great-Grandma's lace: beautiful, thin, frail, and easily unraveled. The frictionless gospel that evangelicalism taught us to recite was nothing more than words and misplaced intentions.

The picture I have painted may be bleak and dreary, but there was tremendous vibrancy, joy, and connection during those years. I released my ignorant understandings of the world. I guess we'd call this dying to myself. Just as violence was prevalent, so too were movements of restoration. I learned something that no Sunday service or message from the pulpit could teach me: the gospel is not a fairytale of individual salvation. It is a liberation story that is still being written. Like many other liberation texts, it is riddled with cautionary tales meant to teach us what we shouldn't do in order for us to pursue a better future. From the garden of Eden to the exodus, from the promised land to the exile, from the Palestinian colonization by Rome to the freedom cries heard in the new heaven and the new earth—every stage of the Bible speaks to our resistance, our weaknesses, and the many ways we have failed each other in our collective liberation from interpersonal sin and institutional oppression.

Through those years God set me up for a life of prophetic disruption. While that's a very fancy term, I think prophetic disruption is the ability to plainly say, "This is problematic." It stems from an innate desire to see past the facade, find the violence, and expose it for the purposes of restoration. Prophetic disruption does not focus on the actions of traumatized individuals. Instead, it looks at why people are reacting and what they are responding to. Violence can be relational, or the atmosphere can be violent. Prophetic disruption is having the ability to understand how both are intertwined in their own proverbial dance of death.

An added layer of prophetic disruption is understanding abuse and trauma in an intimate manner. It begins with asking the right questions. Trauma-informed specialists (whether therapists, caregivers, teachers, or ministers) don't ask, "What's wrong with you?" Instead, we ask, "What happened to you?" Prophetic disruption means that one must exist within that key question, sleuthing and piecing together the stories of violence in order to find the pathway to restoration. Our question—"What happened?"—asks for many things: the personal account, history, identities, community, quantitative data, governance, money trail, and lore held within the situation. It is the intricate braid of critical thought, cultural analysis, and theology.

I wish I could tell you that God magically called me out of that role and into incarnational ministry. It didn't happen that way. When George Floyd was murdered by a bloodthirsty police officer and the system of institutional violence toward Black bodies that supported it, I stopped believing that Christianity was salvific. I listened as people justified his death. I was silenced or shamed for speaking out. I watched people—specifically white people—engage in a range of responses, from willful ignorance to vainly "checking in on me" to appease their consciences. I was beyond exhausted. I was enraged to have given my all to a faith system that justified the death of a Black man and therefore my own death and the death of my children. I felt betrayed by the people who told me they loved me. I received their frictionless gospel in these moments and faced the heart-wrenching truth that the entire foundation given to me was made of sand.

Something just as important happened: no one spoke of Breonna Taylor. I would go to a service at a white evangelical church and hear lies and foolish arguments about George Floyd's life. But no one spoke of Breonna. I was asked to lead "racial reconciliation" trainings in churches and to participate in community racial justice programs. But no one spoke of Breonna. No one knew the names of Sandra Bland, Yuvetter Henderson, or Oluwatoyin Salau. And there was no evidence that they wanted to know these women. Then on March 16, 2021, my hope in Christianity fell apart when eight people, including six Asian women, were murdered by a Christian terrorist emboldened by the abusive teachings of purity culture. We were already steeped in the escalated levels of anti-Asian hate as we watched our Asian elders brutalized in public. It was devastating. What made it more exhausting was experiencing Christians center the victims' sex work over their lives and how we in the Asian American community were so desperate to humanize the victims. Though it felt like continuous punches in the gut, it somehow made sense to me. Christianity celebrates converting the biblical prostitutes, not protecting them. The theologies that we embrace become our lived realities.

There will always be danger in the spaces where silence and igno-rance are favored. I was trying to get people to see the injustice done to the bodies of Black and non-Black people of color. But the theol-ogy limited any hopes of safety or liberation because the theology centered cisgender men. I realized that I existed to theologize and minister myself into silence. I was a pawn for a Christianity that did not want to see me in anything other than a supporting role. Being Black and Asian made me important enough to be invited to sit at their wobbly tables, but being a woman meant that listening to my opinion was a last resort. I was stuck in the intersection of gender and race; my presence was requested but my voice was not necessary. I learned how to boost Christianity by standing still and looking pretty in the name of racial reconciliation. My body was used for market-ing; my voice was never heard. I was being groomed into becoming a concubine for the Western church's flaccid attempts at pursuing racial reconciliation. I was exhausted.

As I processed my feelings with a friend, she said something I'll never forget: "Church folk told us about the Rock of Salvation, but it has been broken down into so many pieces that it's completely useless." Deeply entrenched in my trauma and rage, I realized that my image of Christ was rooted in a patriarchal, white supremacist Jesus that needed to be exposed and burned in the trenches of the hell that it had clawed its way out of. I had to know myself and all the ways I exist as a human being worthy of protection and care. I also had to know the ways that I—a Black and Asian woman—am groomed and targeted to experi-ence violence and erasure. I had to create a theology for myself that stopped centering Christ's triumphant victory and proclaimed survival in the face of constant and unending violence done to my body and the bodies of siblings who are marginalized in a society created for cisgender heteronormative imperialist middle- to upper-class white men.

Approaching Scripture

I believe holy texts do not provide us with answers; instead, they pro-vide an invitation to find our own narratives and ask deeper questions. To believe in the infallibility of leaders and trust in their interpreta-tion without questioning will only lead to destruction. Discernment, curiosity, and accountability are necessary parts of any relationship, so why do we leave it out of our relationship with our holy texts and spiritual leaders? Scripture is the space where questions, callouts, and clapbacks are welcomed.

I am free from the time in my life when blind allegiance, nationalism, and gaslighting dominated my spirituality. I'm glad to see many others on their emancipation journey from oppressive and repressive forms of Christianity. Now we are seeking truth, telling our truth, and letting the truth transform this corrupted institution known as the church. It requires us to silence the dominant voice and understand Bible stories in contexts that aren't rooted in a frictionless gospel. We're taught to cling to biblical stories of triumphant victory and let them guide our way. But these narratives favor the privileged, the racist, the patriarchal, the sexist, the supremacist, and the one who assimilates to their systems of violence. What if the narrative of the gospel is not about the urgency to achieve grandiose victory? What if it's about finding ourselves and each other in trauma's abyss and finding our path to a liberation that heals all wounds and constructs God's kingdom? We've had a couple millennia of irresponsible interpretations and countless exposés of church leaders. It's about time we start believing victims and understanding their path toward healing. Let's start with reclaiming biblical narratives.

If you're looking for a book that dives deep into complex theologies or does contortion performances with biblical translation, know that this book won't do that. My hope is that as we deconstruct our relationship with Scripture and our proximity to Christianity, we give ourselves permission to see our stories within the verses. It is so often taught that the Bible transcends or is triumphant over culture. I don't believe that. I believe the Bible is a book of truth, but truth isn't about having the right answers; it's about finding ourselves in the journey and knowing that we do not struggle alone. This book isn't the pursuit of a holy answer. Rather, it's the reclamation of the way a story can heal us.

A Note on Frameworks

It is important to note that this journey through reclaiming narrative is informed by the intersections of my identity and my own experience of healing from trauma and journeying alongside people who have experienced high levels of trauma. I am a cishet female in a patriarchal society. I am mixed race in a culture that prefers monolithic models of identity. I am Black and Filipina in a society built by whiteness. I am a queer-affirming, poor, second-generation American, first-generation college student, and survivor of violence. I am a minister, educator, and storyteller. These parts of my identity help guide the way these stories are interpreted.

Since I do not seek to give whiteness or patriarchy a footing in this book, I want to take this opportunity to explain the cultural frameworks in which I interpret Scripture. As a Black woman I am rooted in the social theory and praxis of womanism. As a Filipina I am rooted in the Filipinx* psychological pursuit of *kapwa*. I identify as a kapwa womanist. Lastly, I am an abolitionist. Allow me to geek out about these frameworks with you.

Womanism is a social theory and theological framework rooted in the lived experiences of Black women. It's important to know that Blackness and womanness are not monolithic. Both encompass a wide range. Womanism speaks for cisgender Black women, transgender Black women, and those who are Black and identify as nonbinary or gender expansive. Womanism expands beyond social theory into theological framework in how it centers Black women and, as social psychologist Christena Cleveland says, "The womanists don't give a shit about the consensus or the Church's beliefs or what the sacred texts *supposedly* say."[4] I've heard it said that womanism isn't "regular theology" because it deviates from the white male gaze. That thinking is an example of the oppressive force of cultural imperialism. It's also a load of crap. To assume that the white male gaze is "regular theology" is to align oneself with the ethics of colonizers, enslavers, and rapists. It's also important to understand how womanism is separate from the whiteness of feminism. The focal point of feminism is equity based on gender and class. This pursuit focuses on gaining

*There is controversy surrounding the term *Filipinx*. I use the word *Filipinx* to describe people who are from the Philippines. It is a gender-inclusive word. Because my mom's first language, Tagalog, is a genderless language I believe the term *Filipinx* aligns closest with the structure of Tagalog. I will use *Filipina* when referring to a woman or a group of women.

equal power, but since feminism originates from white bourgeoisie women, it specifically centers their pursuit of power. From this vantage point, feminism isn't a liberative pursuit because it centers women who are white, cisgender, and upper class. Womanism, however, analyzes the intersections of gender, race, and class to understand how to dismantle systems of power to create a care-oriented community-based society.

Kapwa is a study born of *Sikolohiyang Pilipino* (Filipinx psychology) that beckons Filipinx peoples in and out of the diaspora to return to the consciousness of our indigenous ancestry.[5] The pursuit of kapwa is an active stance against coloniality, Western rugged individualism, and American militarization happening within the Filipinx consciousness both in and out of the diaspora. Kapwa psychology promotes the interconnection and shared dignity among land and people. As educator Maharaj Desai explains, kapwa stands firmly on three pillars: humanization, our *diwata* (spirituality), and giving voice to muted and marginalized peoples. Kapwa asserts how deep connection between our inner selves and others will develop commitment to community. Critical kapwa pedagogy is the praxis of individuals and communities coming together to pursue collective healing.

Abolition is the work of dismantling and rebuilding. In abolition we dismantle systemic oppression that leads to the trafficking of human beings by way of indentured servitude, domestic labor, colonization, sexual violence, and incarceration. However, abolition is just as much a daily interpersonal endeavor as it is an institutional revolution. Abolitionists question and challenge carceral logics, which are the many ways we perpetuate ideas and practices of policing and imprisonment. To police people is to use force and intimidation to maintain an unequitable status quo that perpetuates harmful power dynamics. I pursue what Sarah Lamble calls "everyday abolition." As she explains, "Everyday abolition means undoing the cultural norms and mindsets that trap us within punitive [punishment-based] habits and logics."[6] Abolitionists are people actively building a new society that centers restoration, repair, accountability, equity, and human flourishing.

This book is a wrestling and reclaiming. It is a space that honors survivors and seeks to help us see our stories in overlooked biblical narratives. This book is about believing victims, understanding harm, and being present in pain to know what healing can look like. The Bible is a liberation text, but to know it and love it as such we must see the narratives from the eyes of those who experienced the most harm. I invite you to join me here.

Unclench your jaw.

Drop your shoulders.

Take a deep breath.

Let's begin.

Chapter One

Eve

"Have you eaten from the tree of which I commanded you not to eat?" The man said, "The woman whom you gave to be with me, she gave me fruit from the tree, and I ate." Then the LORD God said to the woman, "What is this that you have done?" The woman said, "The serpent tricked me, and I ate." . . . To the woman [the LORD God] said,
"I will make your pangs in childbirth exceedingly great;
in pain you shall bring forth children,
yet your desire shall be for your husband,
and he shall rule over you."

—Gen. 3:11–13, 16

Banished Woman Blues

no glass out there in Eden
no lies for us to feed in
don't need it when you're transparent

I was made from that man's ribs
a bone-scrapped blessing been my dibs
I stopped hiding in *ezer kenegdo*

wretched ol' snake got me good
got me good cuz he knew he could
bit me right in the curiosity

no glass out there in Eden
no lies for us to feed in
don't need it when you're transparent

never seen God's face filled with tears
held each other and named our fears
watched skies coagulate under a curse

gave us food, clothes, and all our sorrow
God readied us for a new tomorrow
exile'll teach you to trust yourself

no glass out there in Eden
no lies for us to feed in
don't need it when you're transparent

Blame

I have few memories of my childhood before I turned six. Some of the remaining memories come from spending my weekends in a rundown apartment building on Linden Avenue in the city of Long Beach, California. That was where I spent my days with my mom, her siblings, and my many cousins. My mom immigrated from the Philippines in 1978, two years after her older siblings immigrated by way of American imperialism. My two oldest uncles left the family home in rural Batangas and were recruited into the US Navy.

My mother's side of the family had the good misfortune of being from an island archipelago that the United States strategically used as its oldest military ally in Asia. The Philippines became a US colony after the United States defeated Spain in the Spanish-American War in 1898. Without any say in our own governance, our country of more than 7,000 islands was delivered to the US military. It was then that the United States began recruiting Filipinx nationals into its Navy.

Filipinx peoples looking to escape the crushing poverty imposed by colonialism could escape their impoverished conditions by joining the military power partially responsible for those conditions. Since the 1900s, Filipinx sailors in the US Navy have fought in every US conflict. By 1947 the United States and the Philippines signed a military bases agreement allowing the United States military to occupy the Philippines and create a pathway of recruitment that could eventually lead to citizenship and sponsorship for the Filipinx people seeking the American dream. My mother's two oldest brothers were among the 34,620 Filipinx sailors who were recruited into the US Navy between 1952 and 1990.[1] Upon gaining citizenship, my two uncles sponsored my grandmother and their two additional brothers and their wives for US citizenship. Once my grandmother gained her citizenship, she sponsored her three daughters and three other sons, allowing them to have a pathway to US citizenship. Together they were twelve in total. My family, in pursuit of the American dream, understood that it wouldn't satisfy the soul if it was done alone. They created a pathway that centered on their staying together.

They were a tight-knit immigrant family from a coconut and sugarcane farm in rural Batangas living in one of the busiest industrialized port cities in a global superpower. Together they navigated through this new country, built careers, started relationships, ended relationships, and raised families. Of course, they had the all-too-trusted underground network of Filipinx immigrants who imbued wisdom and resources to them. I was born ten years after my mom immigrated to the United States. By that time on her immigrant journey she had gained decades' worth of lessons, losses, and achievements. One thing was certain: they stayed together.

My mom dropped me off at my lola's apartment on Linden Avenue, and I would spend my day with her. I would pray with my lola, watch her clean the house, and watch *The Price Is Right* and daytime soap operas with her. She'd give me some *pan de sal* to dip into my coffee (that was purposely saturated with too much creamer), for snack I'd have rice with sugar, and for dinner we'd have saimin or rice with canned Vienna sausages. The highlight was unfiltered time with Lola. The apartment on Linden Avenue housed my mom's four brothers. Her sisters lived within a short five-mile drive to this family headquarters. We weren't too far away from each other. At any given moment I could walk upstairs into my Uncle Ninoy's apartment, ask Tito Rollie and Tita Tess if I could play with my cousin, walk downstairs to pay a visit to my Uncle Uping and Aunty Sonia, or be really annoying to my *ates* and *kuyas*. When related and nonrelated family members visited, we'd spend our time together talking exuberantly in Lola's apartment, singing karaoke, and eating. We were together all the time. Within that group were the children of the sisters; our aunties and uncles affectionately called us "the original six." Most weekends our other cousins from San Jose would visit and turn us six into eight.

I am the youngest of our cousin group. I tended to bumble behind my *ates*, annoy my *kuyas* as they played their Nintendo games, get into useless arguments, be the butt of most pranks, or wander off in my imagination. These were the few things I learned from those years: no one can make *tapa* as perfectly crispy as Lola, I can accidentally render parties silent when I scream all the bad words in Tagalog at the top of my lungs, and our family stays together. Who I am—my creation myth—begins with those weekends on Linden Avenue.

Our creation myths are love stories allowing us to choose who we are.

When I think of the story of Adam and Eve, I don't think too much of Eden or the curse. Instead, I think of an immigrant family learning to survive in exile, existing in a land that is east of their Eden. The Philippines has a unique ecosystem. It holds two-thirds of the world's biodiversity and maintains 5 percent of the world's flora. There is no place in the world like our archipelago, and yet the islands are heavily exploited for their natural resources; dictatorships take advantage of our economy; and our *kababayan* struggle to earn a livable wage. Over 6,000 Filipinx people emigrate daily in search of the possibility of a better life.[2] I think of my mom's side of the family making a new way when the comforts of the homeland were not easily attainable. I think of what it means to make a home while referring to another land as Home. There are two homes in a Filipinx family. The first is the home with a lowercase *h*: the place where we leave our shoes at the door, lay our heads, and sit at the table to eat. The second, home with a capital *H*, is the country we had to leave and also the country we long to return to. I learned how to tune my ears to know which word was being used. *Is your dad at home? We're going Home in December. Anak, don't forget to bring these home. Nieneh, I just came back from Home.* In this way of covert language, we remembered that our hearts belong to the soil of the Philippines.

Being the American-born child of an immigrant family gives me a different reality from that of my mom and her siblings. My Black father from the Mississippi Delta gifted me with an entirely different knowledge of this country. My own American experience was hard for my mom and her siblings to understand. How can a child explain what it means to see the world from two continents? What remained true in our cross-cultural and multigenerational experience is the same: no matter the circumstances, we belonged together. Conflicts may have been many and multilayered, but that didn't change the truth of those early years. I belonged to this family of Filipinx immigrants who learned how to belong to this new country.

The United States has much to offer, but it is not Home. I often think of Adam—formed of the swirling dust and soil—longing to return to the land that knows him.

There was a time when I believed Adam and Eve were our first ancestors. People would proclaim that we all come from the same bloodline. They'd spout beliefs that racism or sexism or any -ism couldn't exist because we're all related. I was told that it was ungodly and demonic to operate outside of colorblindness because that would disrespect the first man and woman and, in doing so, would blaspheme God.

"We are all the same," said the liars and gaslighters, "because we are all children of Adam and Eve."

I stopped clinging to that belief the moment those people demanded that I assimilate to a theology that requires me to erase my identity to melt into an oppressive norm. It's a pity how those people talked of blood and bone but said nothing of their own punishment-based systems, their bloodlust, and the ways they demand a pound of flesh every time they felt their way of life was threatened. It upsets me when people try to trace our ancestry back to Adam and Eve while completely disregarding the violence done throughout these generations. People want the beauty of the myth, but they can't handle the harsh reality that comes with accountability and reconciliation. I love and struggle with creation myths; people will cling to the parts that serve their intentions and proclaim them as evidence for their justifications. But I do it as well; I use my myth to hide the pain of a childhood laden with violence. Our myths are not fact; they are convenience. Many times they are the fuel that keeps us alive. The problem is that when a myth becomes fact we lose the part of our humanity that allows us to be connected and find restoration through a beautiful story.

I think the creation myth of the Hebrew Bible is a story that is both beautiful and ugly, but I don't think it's true. Instead, it is a tapestry made for survival, because this is what a good story can do: it can keep us alive as death pursues us. In her book *Inspired: Slaying Giants, Walking on Water, and Loving the Bible Again*, the late Rachel Held Evans wrote that the stories of Genesis are not factual historical accounts but a collective remembering of a people—exiled, lost, and frantically searching for freedom—gathering together and bearing witness to the multifaceted character of God. Evans writes of how the origin story of Adam and Eve provides us with questions that help us cling to hope when all that surrounds us is devastation. This understanding changed my relationship with Scripture. I used to be in Christian communities that proclaimed the Bible to be a factual text that could not be questioned or challenged. White men would put their hands

on their Bibles and say that it was God's holy text. Black men would
hold it up in the air and say that it is the only truth of life. White
women would claim the Bible stands for "*basic instructions before
leaving Earth.*" Those same people would use these texts to justify,
blame, bind, and shame me. They called this love and expected me to
be obedient to their sorry excuse for love. It's sad how a survival story
becomes a control narrative in the hands of manipulative people.

Allowing myself to break free from a rigid view of the Hebrew
Bible gave me permission to take ownership of myself. Knowing
these stories were passed down from person to person, I see the ways
in which hope is kept alive and lessons are shared. My immigrant
family members will tell stories of Home and leave behind bread-
crumbs of warnings to help me understand why colonization, militarization, and corrupt government officials are the reason why we
stay in the United States. What I see in this story of exile is a sequence
of "bewares" meant to keep us alive and together in the face of the
violence we are facing:

> Beware of the cunning serpent who asks many questions and
> leads you to distrust the family; the serpent will change your
> mind and leave you standing naked and alone (Gen. 3:1).
> Beware of the knowledge that tastes sweet but will lead us to
> destruction (Gen. 3:4).
> Beware of the ways you want to blame others instead of seeking
> accountability for your own wrongdoings (Gen. 3:12).
> Beware of the consequences to your actions, for your harm-
> ful actions will curse both the people and the earth (Gen.
> 3:17–19).
> Beware of the many ways a heart can be broken and a people
> can be exiled (Gen. 3:22).
> Beware, because when one person does harm, the whole com-
> munity will suffer.

The story of Adam and Eve breaks my heart. They are the first
immigrant family—two people crafted and nurtured by the hands
of a God who revels in creating harmony-based communities that
cross species, sexes, and divinity, a God so devoted to community as

to prefer the plural pronoun *us.* "Let us make humans in our image" (Gen. 1:26). Adam and Eve have everything they need in this place of wonder. Eve listens to a serpent who tells her that she can gain more and live better, to chase a dream that can only exist outside of God's ecosystem. She puts her trust in the serpent's words and does as he said, eating the fruit of knowledge. Eve savors possibility and shares its deliciousness with Adam. Realization injects itself into the place of possibility, and they find their nakedness—their ways of existing within their home—to be shameful.

God finds them hiding and realizes that they've eaten the fruit and that they no longer love their ways of existing in his world. God asks Adam what happened, and Adam blames Eve. "The woman whom you gave to be with me—she gave me fruit from the tree, and I ate" (3:12). God watches the children They created turn away from the love that formed them. I imagine God's shoulders slumped and eyes filled with tears as They expressed Their disappointment and feelings of betrayal. Unable to trust Adam and Eve, God curses the humans and exiles the pair from the place of nourishment—but first God sews clothes and gives provision. Adam and Eve are banished but not evicted. They are forcibly removed from their unique ecosystem and become immigrants in a land that is east of all they know.

Woven throughout is blood and bone, mucus and orgasms, exile and loneliness, devastation and survival. At its center is the way the first humans betray God, the blame Adam places on Eve, and the blame God places on Adam. We read this story and see the destruction of community. Once community is destroyed, the *imago Dei* is damaged, becoming more and more fractured until all that's left are the shrapnel shells of destruction an ego-driven humanity leaves behind. I have been taught to read their story and use it to sow division and blame. I rebuke that teaching. Instead, I wish we could learn to use these lessons to create a pathway for restoration. With a broken heart, I ask myself, *What does it mean for us to return to Eden? What does it mean to collectively come back Home?*

It's ironic that the Bible says all humankind is made in the image of God, yet our practices suggest anything but that. Generations of preachers have spewed hatred and contempt toward Eve and every other body that is not a cisgender male. In their eyes, women are the initiators of original sin—made solely to be blamed so that the patriarchy can remain the standard. Isn't it ironic that the stories told to keep us bound in belonging to Christ are used to divide and conquer our very souls? What's more disappointing are the responses created in the circles of so-called Christian feminism, born in the minds of conservative white bourgeois women who subscribe to the violent powermongering that defines patriarchy. There is no liberation in their interpretations. They are dedicated to upholding standards of patriarchy and complementarianism. They believe proclaiming the worthiness of womanhood is the only way to combat the violence of blame. I've heard their disappointing statements, and there was a time when I believed in them:

"Women are the crowning jewel of creation."
"You are the life-giving *ezer kenegdo*."
"Daughter of God, you were bought with a price."

There's no liberation in objectification. It's taken me too long to learn that. I'm exhausted of women's ministries that are driven by proclaiming purpose instead of advocating for our humanity. If I must prove that I and my kin are useful, then our community lacks the *imago Dei*. God gave me very high standards for what community means; I want no less than the *imago Dei*.

Is it too much to demand something else besides a Christian blame narrative? Ours is a spirituality that sings of the spilled blood and water of Christ, but relegates the blood and water pouring out of the bodies of menstruating people as nothing more than a curse. There's something uniquely holy and agonizing within the bodies of people with periods. It's too bad these revelations are muted and denied. We watch sermons that center the cishet male experiences, read scientific tests done on cishet men, or listen to podcasts that favor the cishet man. Those of us holding other identities are expected to follow along. But what about the people who have periods? What of our blood theology speaks toward our humanity and rebukes the ways patriarchal women are convinced to prove our usefulness?

I was told the first blood spilled on the earth was Abel's, as he was killed by his brother Cain. But when I reread this story, I think of the bloody show that signifies the beginning of labor. It's what happens at the end of pregnancy to prepare the womb for labor. What if the first blood that the earth knew of was from birth and not murder? Eve's body releasing its womb blood was a necessary sacrifice to welcome new life into their exiled world—but there is more to birth than blood. It is blood, water, mucus, pain, and heaving breathless joy.

I love to spend my time thinking about how the theology of blood can pen our resistance narratives. Eve's blood being spilled in birth is in direct opposition to the militaristic rule of the Babylonian Empire. The essence of the first birth—blood, water, mucus, pain—exists generations later in the torture and death of the Christ. Like Eve, the spilling of Jesus' blood is a form of resistance to a militaristic empire. Ancient Western Asian literary art used blood as a tool to express militaristic might. The tribes and empires of ancient Western Asia celebrated the ways their enemies were injured, bloodied, and extinguished. Blood imagery was a tool to uphold the values of violence and conquest in patriarchal empires. Depictions of men and war needed to show spilled blood and severed body parts to establish the rule of power: the transformation of the Nile waters to blood (Exod. 7:14–25), Samson slaying a thousand men with a donkey's jawbone (Judg. 15:16), and David delivering 200 foreskins (1 Sam. 18:27). Associating blood with death and victory meant female blood must stay hidden. To bleed and live is to challenge patriarchy, and clearly we can't have that in our ancient texts. Blood being used to establish power objectifies the victim. Eve is a victim of Adam's blame, but her blood defies victimhood because she does not die from his accusations. Instead, her blood brings new life into the world. Her blood is resistance to patriarchy.

Jesus being the embodied word of God takes this blood theology from the creation myth further when he offers his metaphorical blood at the Last Supper. Jesus uses the metaphorical language of spilled blood, drawing from the male-centered images of torturous murder and the feminine imagery of giving life through food and feast. In using imagery associated with femininity, Jesus gives us a multilayered understanding of blood: it proclaims his divinity, foretells his traumatic crucifixion, and asserts the humanity of period-having people. Jesus transgressed gender through his blood by favoring the life-giving imagery associated with Eve, the first human to give life. The blood of the communion is about fertility—the essence of life—instead of the traditionally patriarchal pursuit of conquest.[3] For menstruating people, ours is a blood flow that cannot be controlled or contained.

In Scripture, our blood flow is used as a metaphor of impurity; touching menstrual blood merits punishment. But there are two types of impurity in Scripture: sacral impurity is the consequence of a natural phenomenon, like menstruating; moral impurity results from acts of violence. Cleansing ourselves from sacral impurity doesn't serve to remove shame but to wash away excess blood, sweat, and stink. Bathing isn't bad. Patriarchy, however, doesn't give us time to disentangle the two forms of impurity. Instead, it consolidates the two, allowing our bodies to be objectified and our identities to be dehumanized: the menstruating body is impure, as are all the things it touches (Lev. 15:19–24); the punishment for sex during menstruation is isolation (Lev. 20:18); and idolatry in Israel is described as being as impure as menstrual blood (Ezek. 36:17).

Jesus disentangles what was consolidated. He restores sacral purity rituals through Communion. It's important to recognize how Jesus uses images of offering and suffering to establish our intimacy with divinity. When I was a little girl growing up in the Roman Catholic Church, I would admire the adults who were allowed to drink the sacrificial wine during mass. I thought it was a big honor to be able to drink that Jesus juice and know Christ in that way. (Like many kids, I later learned that it tastes awful.) Tired of waiting for my First Communion to happen, I simply asked my mom why it was so important to drink from that cup of (metaphorical) blood. Her answer was simple: "It helps us remember God."

Blood holds life and memory. I am even more delighted to contemplate how the metaphorical blood of the Communion is transgendered blood made to affirm the humanity of women as well as trans and gender-expansive peoples.

Beyond the pain and inconvenience of our periods, menstruating people have a different relationship with how our blood holds life and memory. There's a correlation between our cycles of blood and the way our bodies hold trauma. Unfortunately, most research on posttraumatic stress disorder (PTSD) is done with male war veterans.

It details trauma as an experience associated with the violence of battle, taking attention away from the ways that women's bodies can experience violence and hold it in. A 2011 study of estradiol, a major female sex hormone involved in the regulation of the menstrual cycle, revealed that when the menstruating body approaches ovulation, it will experience more symptoms related to PTSD. The follicular phase (which starts on the first day of blood until ovulation) elevates estradiol levels and signals different events that prepare the body for ovulation. Once ovulation begins, the estradiol level lowers and activates the limbic system. The limbic system of the brain supports the functions that include our emotions, behavior, and long-term memory. As the limbic system activates and moves us into a fear response (fight, flight, freeze, or faint), the prefrontal cortex—which is responsible for functioning control, attention, impulse, and cognitive flexibility—lowers cognitive control. In other words, as the emotional center of our brains rises, our bodies loosen their capacity to control how we process that emotional content. Stress and anxiety heighten, and we experience greater fear responses.[4]

A 2021 women-led study took these findings to understand how it can pertain specifically to people who have experienced PTSD. Researchers studied forty women between the ages of eighteen and thirty-three who had experienced a traumatic event. They conducted the study in two parts: The first was to measure the women's estradiol levels, interview them about their traumatic experiences, and ask them to explain how their PTSD symptoms showed up in the past month. In the second part, the researchers asked the women to spend a ten-day span of time answering five daily questionnaires and completing a PTSD checklist in the evenings. The researchers found that during the low-estradiol days of their cycle, the women had more severe PTSD symptoms.[5]

The sexual violence that lives in our bodies peaks and plunges along with our blood flow. In pouring out his blood, Christ restores the *imago Dei*—the divine model of relational mutuality. Christ reclaimed the imagery of blood willingly spilled, not slayed or sacrificed. Christ needed to transgress gender through his blood because those of us with bodies that pour out blood are intimately connected with remembering suffering. We use this genius to build restorative relationships. The blood is neither shame nor curse but an embodied prayer for renewal, connection, and belonging, begging for our human community to be restored to the *imago Dei.*

I dedicated a portion of my life to being a trauma-informed practitioner who leaned on science to explain how PTSD and complex PTSD (C-PTSD) can show up in people. I've used trauma science to advocate for people and disprove limiting beliefs that marginalize the vulnerable. But I am also leery of science because of the harm done in its name to the bodies of Black and non-Black women of color. Too much of our blood has been violently spilled in the name of science. It is truly demonic how scientists have forcefully experimented on the bodies of Black and non-Black women of color. It feels counterintuitive for me to use science as an instrument of worship knowing that it's been a torture device for us. I believe that the journey of ending sexual violence in Christian contexts also involves understanding how problematic theologies normalized medical oppression on our bodies. In order to reclaim our theological understandings in liberative ways, we must be aware of what evils arose and how we can stop them from perpetuating.

In her book *Medical Apartheid: The Dark History of Medical Experimentation on Black Americans from Colonial Times to the Present,* Harriet A. Washington gives the first written account detailing 400 years of medical experimentation done on enslaved and oppressed Black peoples. With historical evidence, she explains how medical practitioners believed the lie that Black people were subhuman objects that didn't feel pain, and so science experiments were conducted on them.[6] But what are the origins of this lie that turned into belief?

In the 1787 manual *Treatise on Tropical Diseases,* Dr. Benjamin Mosely asserted that Black people could bear surgical operations more easily than white people and, therefore, didn't need to have the same accommodations that white people did. Furthermore, he claimed that Black bodies had weaker lungs and needed to remain subject to "intensive labor" for their organs to strengthen.[7]

These racist beliefs and practices persisted into the nineteenth century, exemplified in the heinously violent works of Dr. James Marion Sims, who is known as "the father of modern gynecology" but was truly nothing more than a sadistic misogynoir. He achieved his medical breakthroughs by conducting dehumanizing procedures on enslaved Black women without anesthesia. One detailed account described the sheer evil of his works: "Each naked anaesthetized slave woman had to be forcibly restrained by the other physicians through her shrieks of agony as Sims determinedly sliced, then sutured her genitalia. The other doctors fled when they could bear the scene no longer. It then fell on the [Black] women to restrain one another."[8] Sims's work of torturing Black female bodies earned him accolades in the medical field, eventually leading to his becoming president of the American Medical Association.

Black women's bodies became the site of multiple curses: the curse of blame perpetuated by the story of Adam and Eve's exile, the curse of dehumanization through the lens of white supremacy, and the curse of muting our pain through medical apartheid. There has yet to be a reckoning in the medical field to demand that Black women's bodies be respected. To this day, Black women are three times more likely to die from a pregnancy-related cause than white women.[9] Black women have shorter life expectancies and are disproportionately at risk for chronic illnesses such as anemia, cardiovascular disease, and diabetes.[10] Black women are blamed for health disparities that have been caused by generational trauma, medical biases, and enforced powerlessness from the socioeconomic climate of this country built on misogynoir. The lie persists to this day. In 2017 a medical student shared photos of a textbook from London-based publisher Pearson Education. The photos were of a section entitled "Cultural Differences in Response to Pain," which circulated the same old racist and sexist lie that nonwhite bodies are more resistant to pain.[11]

Theologies built on dehumanizing lies result in cultures built on a foundation of hatred. Entire empires were erected and established on a theology of curse and blame. It was the double dose of hatred of the female body and the Black body that developed systems of medical knowledge supporting the subjugation and torture of Black women's bodies. Non-Black women of color also bear the impact of medical racism. Indigenous women and Latinas have been victims of forced sterilizations to ensure the flourishing of white Christian nationalism within the United States.[12] Violence against Asian American and

Pacific Islander (AAPI) women—fueled by white Christian nationalism's xenophobic ideologies and the cultural oversexualization of AAPI women—is a factor that directly explains why AAPI women are the least likely to get a cervical cancer screening.[13] We are the givers of life and receivers of brutality. Hidden deep within our bodies are the lies of an empire so fragile that it needs us to internalize blame and accept torture in order for it to flourish.

I was raised in a Christianity that built whole theologies on lies, blame, and dehumanization. I was told to look at the story of Adam and Eve to know the downfall of humanity and to focus my attention on Adam blaming Eve in front of God. But what of Eve? The curse God gave was done to her body, and therefore her journey through exile was to rebuke shame and find goodness in her body as the pathway back to God. It is not lost on me that Eve is the first one to speak of God after being exiled from Eden. After birthing Cain she glorifies God, saying, "I have produced a man with the help of the Lord" (Gen. 4:1). Here she proclaims that God remains with her though she does not live in Eden, their Home. This acknowledgment is a statement of defiance against the narrative of blame that was given to her by Adam and perpetuated through patriarchy. Advocacy is Eve's chosen song of worship given to the Lord.

To participate in advocacy is to practice belonging. Eve had to learn how to belong to herself as she pursued a restorative relationship with Adam. When God gave the terms of the curse, They changed the land and altered her body. Adam's curse was a difficult task: he is held accountable, then rendered powerless. God revokes Adam's dominion over the land, humbling him so that he learns how to cooperate with it and to develop a relationship that restores the dignity of the woman he blamed. I believe God's curse was meant to restore us to safety, but we've been so busy blaming each other that we don't even know what it means.

I learned how to worship through self-advocacy when I was pregnant with my third child. I ended up in the emergency room after the births of my first two children. Both times, my birth workers blamed me for my hospitalization. The message was clear: The pain, infection, and illness happened because of me. I was at fault.

I decided to pursue a different avenue for birthing my third child and sought care with a team of nursing midwives at a local birth center that worked in tandem with obstetricians from the local hospital. This pregnancy was mired with the stress from two traumatic birth experiences, the constant exposure to violence and police brutality that led to the 2020 racial protests, and the isolation of living in those early months of the pandemic. I was trying to survive each day and ensure that my baby would make it to term. I worked diligently to ensure that I was surrounded by a birth team who would empathize with my pain and wouldn't blame me as my previous midwife did. Creating this birth team of empathetic and engaged professionals was my first step toward self-advocacy, because I knew my pregnancy journey would lead me to places where I had no language to express what was happening with my body. My team was primarily made of Black women: my doula, who spoke with me once a week to help me set my mindset for birth; the nursing-midwife at the birth center whom I entrusted myself to; my gynecologist; and our pediatrician. It was empowering to have women who believed my pain because they knew the disparities within the system and heard stories like mine.

When I developed cholestasis and my pregnancy turned high risk, the team of nursing-midwives at my birth center laid out all the information and helped me make a plan that was centered on informed consent. When I expressed worries about solidifying boundaries to protect my mental health, my doula helped me create affirmations that I could use to remind myself that my boundaries were sacred. When our newborn son had abnormally high bilirubin levels and had to be taken to the ER for jaundice treatment, his pediatrician called me regularly to check on his health and to soothe me. I am usually unafraid to advocate for myself and others—but those natural skills and abilities are nullified when I have to navigate through the medical field as a Black woman traumatized by horrendous postpartum experiences in this time in history when the death of Black birthing mothers is three times higher than that of white birthing mothers.[14] For me, self-advocacy looked like having a team of people who would not allow blame and misogynoir to ruin my birth or endanger my baby's health. In creating my birth team, I learned how to belong to my body after blame nearly stole my life. In the most frightening parts of my pregnancy, it was Eve's story that anchored me in the knowledge that advocacy and trust will lead us Home. Eden was the place of safety, our first Home. It could not handle the conflict of betrayal. Betrayal and blame set fire to the goodness of advocacy and belonging. Safety cannot exist when betrayal and blame loom in the atmosphere. Our return to Home is not the return to a magical place; it is the return to felt safety that gives us belonging in this violent world. This great journey toward belonging is multi-layered; we are learning how to belong to ourselves, to each other, and to the earth. Belonging can only exist in the places where blame is suffocated.

Chapter Two

Hagar

Now Sarai, Abram's wife, bore him no children. She had an Egyptian slave whose name was Hagar, and Sarai said to Abram, "You see that the LORD has prevented me from bearing children; go in to my slave; it may be that I shall obtain children by her." And Abram listened to the voice of Sarai. So, after Abram had lived ten years in the land of Canaan, Sarai, Abram's wife, took Hagar the Egyptian, her slave, and gave her to her husband Abram as a wife. He went in to Hagar, and she conceived, and when she saw that she had conceived, she looked with contempt on her mistress. Then Sarai said to Abram, "May the wrong done to me be on you! I gave my slave to your embrace, and when she saw that she had conceived, she looked on me with contempt. May the LORD judge between you and me!" But Abram said to Sarai, "Your slave is in your power; do to her as you please." Then Sarai dealt harshly with her, and she ran away from her.

—Gen. 16:1–6

Memoir of an Occupied Womb, a pantoum

Skin richer than soil, body poorer than fields in drought,
I suppose my appearance is a reminder of my purpose.
He smiles softly because its hue glows like the God he talks to while
she murmurs incantations, rubbing her navel with dirt.

I suppose my appearance is a reminder of my purpose.
I am a tool for one person's pleasure, another's bidding;
She murmurs incantations, rubbing her navel with dirt.
Call her "wife" not "barren" "used" or "Pharoah's concubine."

I am a tool for one person's pleasure, another's bidding;
The husband adorns her beautifully with jewels and linens.
Call her "wife" not "barren" "used" or "Pharoah's concubine."
She is a centerpiece, his best tool, perfectly poised for his gain;

The husband adorns her beautifully with jewels and linens.
Abram's best currency is the body of his beloved.
She is a centerpiece, his best tool, perfectly poised for his gain;
An offering to be tasted by others, a lie presented as a gift.

Abram's best currency is the body of his beloved.
Songs were written about Sarai's beauty,
An offering to be tasted by others, a lie presented as a gift.
They purchased me, I thought I gained a beautiful mother.

Songs were written about Sarai's beauty,
"There is wonder in your eyes," she said.
They purchased me, I thought I gained a beautiful mother.
"That is too dangerous for a woman to have," she said.

"There is wonder in your eyes," she said.
In those days I did what I could to stay near her.
"That is too dangerous for a woman to have," she said.
Counting my errors seemed to ease her disappointments,

In those days I did what I could to stay near her.
She'd set up hurdles for me to blunder through.
Counting my errors seemed to ease her disappointments,
Each mistake earned blame and blame turned to bruises.

She'd set up hurdles for me to blunder through,
I nursed myself singing songs from mother Egypt.
Each mistake earned blame and blame turned to bruises.
Sarai hated singing; it reminded her of her cruelty.

I nursed myself singing songs from mother Egypt.
Her desperation became bitterness; her bitterness, resignation.
Sarai hated singing; it reminded her of her cruelty.
The ache of her bitterness appeared in the cracks of my body.

Her desperation became bitterness; her bitterness, resignation.
She believed she was the curse bringing pestilence and famine to Egypt:
The ache of her bitterness appeared in the cracks of my body.
"Curses can't get pregnant," she told me. "You must obey me."

She believed she was the curse bringing pestilence and famine to Egypt:
She sacrificed the body of a servant to protect the promise of tomorrow.
"Curses can't get pregnant," she told me. "You must obey me."
"Do not fail the woman who owns you, or the man who enters you."

She sacrificed the body of a servant to protect the promise of tomorrow.
I served my mistress during the day; I pleased her husband at night,
"Do not fail the woman who owns you, or the man who enters you."
She watched for my bloods and stuck her hand in me, waiting for a child.

I served my mistress during the day; I pleased her husband at night,
She wanted a reason to dance, to once again be Sarai of beauty and joy,
She watched for my bloods and stuck her hand in me, waiting for a child.
When my bloods stopped, she danced for everyone.

She wanted a reason to dance, to once again be Sarai of beauty and joy,
All their hardships were answered through my body.
When my bloods stopped, she danced for everyone.
Abram clapped when he saw, knowing full and well what happened,

All their hardships were answered through my body.
My body swelled as the atmosphere between us staled.
Abram clapped when he saw, knowing full and well what happened,
They wanted the pregnancy to be a blessing, it was a prison.

My body swelled as the atmosphere between us staled.
People have breaking points, sorrow swallows joy and violence ensues;
They wanted the pregnancy to be a blessing, it was a prison.
I sat with them in their marriage tent as Abram hummed my song.

People have breaking points, sorrow swallows joy and violence ensues;
I begged every god and every idol I knew to make it stop.
I sat with them in their marriage tent as Abram hummed my song.
"May the wrong done to me be on you!" cried Sarai.

I begged every god and every idol I knew to make it stop.
Abram deflected, knowing he had power in maintaining her safety,
"May the wrong done to me be on you!" cried Sarai.
"Have you forgotten that she is in your power? Do as you wish with her."

Abram deflected, knowing he had power in maintaining her safety,
I cannot receive what she does, there is no shelter for me in their hearts.
"Have you forgotten that she is in your power? Do as you wish with her."
I do not wish to describe to you the pain that she caused me.

I cannot receive what she does, there is no shelter for me in their hearts.
I fled with little: my songs of Egypt, open wounds, and swollen womb.
I do not wish to describe to you the pain that she caused me.
I am fleeing. Unprotected. Pregnant. Watching you hear my story.

Proximity to Power

In the world of human trafficking, the trafficker will compel a victim to abuse, torture, and manipulate other victims until she is psychologically dependent on the person in power. This first victim eventually understands the trafficker's violence as affection and adopts the trafficker's goal. The violence the first victim receives from the trafficker is passed down to a second victim; thus, the same cycle of abuse is emulated in this new relationship. The trafficker does not have to put much effort in abusing the second victim because the first victim is emulating the trafficker's action. In the business of American pimping, this dynamic is known as "having a bottom bitch." Trafficker and business consultant Pimpin' Ken (née Ken Ivy) describes a bottom bitch as "the one [a pimp] will always win with. She's the one who will school all of the other hoes to a pimp's ways. She'll let the other hoes know that if they're not down with the pimp and his ways, they have to leave."[1]

Sarai is Abram's bottom bitch. Her function in their relationship is to ensure his goals are met, and for centuries their story was used to propagate Christian patriarchy. Abram's meet-the-goal-at-any-cost intensity is associated with faith and hope, whereas Sarai embodies fear and doubt. We are told to be unwavering like Abram, because doing so will ensure that we are faithful and that God will produce what is promised. In contrast, Sarai's doubt is the obstacle to Abram's righteous living.

I was once told, "Be an Abram in a world of Sarais." I regard "this versus that" thinking to be lazy theology, because it does not take into account the nuance, the trauma, and the trail of suffering it leaves behind. Binaries are for people who want to pick a team and cheer in the bleachers; they are not for theological insight. We get caught in the binary when we focus on these stale interpretations of Abram and Sarai; patriarchal violence is justified in Abram's actions, and the model of femininity is the one-dimensional pursuit to have offspring. Focusing on two competing forces will not carve the way toward a liberation that heals and uplifts. We need nuance to better understand the story and God's path toward an equitable future that looks more like the kingdom of God and less like the raggedy unjust dynamics we currently have in place.

Hagar is our nuance.

Abram's faithfulness came at the cost of Sarai's body first. He trafficked her to the Egyptian pharaoh to keep himself safe (Gen. 12:10–20). The plan worked: Abram was treated well, given many gifts, and received many servants. As I comb through these verses, I wonder if young Hagar was a gift given to Sarai. Her presence became the symbol of manipulation between the couple. The abuser (Abram) gave his wife (Sarai) a gift (Hagar) after having trafficked her to another man (Pharoah).

Hagar as Sarai's servant also serves Abram's need to justify why his plan worked. Whereas Sarai's body is the currency to keep Abram safe from Pharoah, Hagar's body is the symbol of Abram's manipulative actions. As their story unfolds, God makes it clear that he is unhappy with Abram's actions by inflicting a serious disease on Pharoah and his household. Pharoah summons Abram to demand why the traveler and tribal leader lied about this marital status to Sarai. "What have you done to me?" says Pharoah. "Why didn't you tell me she was your wife? Why did you say, 'She is my sister,' so that I took her to be my wife? Now then, here is your wife. Take her and go!"

What interests me about this confrontation between the two men is how the narrator positions Sarai as the source of the "serious disease." I am not one to indulge in biblical gossip, but I find myself wondering if this "serious disease" is a sexually transmitted infection. If so, then Abram offered his wife as patient zero in the spread of a biblical venereal disease that could—at that time—only be described as a plague. Sarai, being the host of this case of biblical epidemiology, could have possibly contracted this disease elsewhere. Thus, the wrath of God that befell the house of Pharaoh was more like the consequences of Abram's actions of objectifying his wife.

Actions have consequences, and the very real consequence for Abram and Sarai is to be forcefully removed from Egypt with their tribe, their possessions, and their newly acquired collection of servants. Sarai had additional consequences. She was bound to Abram; the safety and privileges their marriage provided her couldn't be replicated elsewhere. Decades before they entered Egypt, Abram told Sarai that God has a promise to fulfill through their marriage. She couldn't leave her husband no matter how poorly he treated her or how often he used her. She stayed and remained in allegiance to the vision God gave him. Enter Hagar. She silently slithers through each scene as a faceless servant within the accounts of Genesis—that is, until Sarai pulls a bottom bitch move and suggests Abram impregnate Hagar. God's promise becomes Abram's vision, which becomes Sarai's goal. At this point Sarai has been married to her trafficker for about seven decades and is bearing the weight of shame that comes with being barren. Sarai trafficking Hagar is reenacting her own abuse because Sarai internalized the violence that Abram allowed to happen to her. Once violence is internalized, it becomes the template for how to engage in other relationships. Sarai, a victim of Abram's actions, is repeating the same abuse of power that her husband had in Egypt twenty years earlier. A hallmark of the bottom bitch is an inability to leave the pimp. Part of this inability results from the normalized violence and manipulation in the relationship that creates a system of dependency. As trafficker Pimpin' Ken puts it:

> Weakness is the best trait a person can find in someone they want to control. If you can't find a weakness, you have to create one. You have to tear someone's ego down to nothing before they will start looking to you for salvation. Then you have a chance to build them back up, showing them that it's your program that takes them from darkness to hope. While you want them to feel good about themselves eventually, you want them to feel that it's because of *you*. They begin to see you as their champion, their hero—even if the weakness you rescue them from is the one you created.[2]

This dynamic in the Abram-Sarai-Hagar relationship is exploitation. Sex is the labor: Sarai was used to fulfill Pharaoh's sexual desire, and Hagar was used to fulfill Abram's goal of having an heir. Sarai, so often characterized as the symbol of doubt, is a victim who—without knowing a better way—chooses the same tactics her husband/trafficker does in order to obtain his goal. Her victim-to-oppressor journey is a common theme in violence: a desperation and scarcity mindset will prevent people from finding a new way, so they regurgitate the same system of power that oppressed them. I call this one's *proximity to power*.

Proximity to power goes beyond human trafficking. Whether it's a bullied student bullying another student, a domestic violence victim using the same tactics on their children, or an employee threatening a coworker in the same tone as their employer—pursuing the proximity to power is a regular theme in all forms of exploitation. Manipulated persons will believe the abuser's narrative in order to survive. Their identity is found in their ability to achieve the goal of the person in power. Internalized violence is how victims hold that identity and how they will continue to justify the necessity of their harmful actions in terms of the overall goal of the abuser. It is irresponsible to believe that traumatized persons can be free from normalized and internalized violence on their own. It takes intervention to imagine a new possibility and create it. Liberation from oppression is found in the intervention and not in repeating these abusive power structures.

Pursuit of proximity to power appears interpersonally in the schoolyard, bedroom, and boardroom, but it also reveals itself in our social movements. Know this: I *am not* saying that every social movement serves the goals of one in power. What I *am* saying is that many social movements are not liberation-based because their goal is either to pursue a watered-down equality that satisfies the status quo and leaves space for future exploitation, or to replace current power with a similar structure and a different person at the top.

Any attempt to gain equal proximity to power will falter. Power is narcissistic, and people who pursue it become fuel to this defining characteristic. Power loves more power and will do what it can to keep the existing power dynamic in place. Attempting to align with the figurehead of power will eventually—whether it is today, tomorrow, or years from now—make you a bottom bitch. After all, the purpose of power is to exploit. When you want to become more like the one in a position of power, you will acclimate your action to theirs.

I recently came across a journal that I had when I was sixteen. A short entry in the beginning caught my eye: *I hate myself. I don't know who I'm going to be, but I want it to be better than who I am now. I want to be someone who is accepted, kind, compassionate, and beautiful.* In the lines that followed I wrote a list of women I admired and who I wanted to be like. Every woman on that list was a white actress. Reading that entry was a searing reminder of my deeply embedded self-hatred. I closed the journal and said a prayer for the sixteen-year-old within me who carried all that internalized violence. As I uttered my completing "Amen," a flood of memories came back. They were traumatic memories that I unknowingly hid within the darkest corners inside my mind. I don't understand the science of it, but I realize that storing these memories away was how my brain chose to protect me from decades of internalized violence.

I recalled the violent details of the household that I grew up in. I remembered how the darkest corners of the closet were the only place I felt safe to cry. I remembered the blame and the shame. I remembered the heart-wrenching fear I had of people who were meant to keep me safe. I remembered being told that I was the problem for things I was too young to understand or control. I remembered my brother once asking me, "Why did you make yourself into a white girl?" when I was creating avatars for a video game.

I remembered the times I was bullied for my hair, how classmates would yell names at me because of my hair texture. I remember begging my mom to get my hair fixed and being told we couldn't afford it. I remember trash being thrown in my hair and unsolicited ignorant hair-care advice being shoved my way. I remember the ways that I would pull at my own hair and cry because it wasn't straight and beautiful.

I heard the offensive screams of my basketball coach, the criticisms and racist comments that came from teachers. I remembered how my classmates would look at me and tell me that I was the stupidest person in the world. I remembered having to defend my personhood and crying because I felt that no one believed me. I remembered all the ways I embraced perfectionism and a false sense of self so that I could be safe in violent places.

I remembered papaya soap and skin-whitening products that family members mailed from the Philippines. I remembered combing my hair until my scalp was numb and crying in the mirror because all that work to comb my hair didn't change how I looked. I remembered being ten years old and sitting in the pews of our Catholic church and asking God to either make it stop or to kill me because I couldn't live like this.

I remembered a childhood filled with violence around every corner and hidden within each corridor. I wept as the memories flooded in, and I grieved for the girl within me. She did not know how to be mad at the systems of violence that surrounded her, so she chose to blame herself.

I internalized white supremacy because I didn't know how to be safe from it. I idolized white women and sought to be like them and look like them because—in my limited understanding—that's what it meant to be accepted in this world. I embraced the self-abuse that came with perfectionism and assimilating to whiteness. I converted to their death-filled forms of Protestant Christianity and began rebuking the faith traditions of my Catholic Filipinx family. I denied my Blackness and believed white Christians who said that Black liberation and womanism were demonic. I was a child. I believed that hurting and blaming myself in the name of a white colonial Jesus was a lesser form of the abuse I experienced from a racist-sexist-classist America. I believe this was how self-acceptance worked because a radical self-love that celebrated every part of my identity was not something that I had the ability to consider.

I was a bottom bitch to white supremacist patriarchy. It took a long time for the violence to stop; by then I had created a persona that thoroughly hated herself. I became this Black and Asian person who was palatable for white people. I grew up in predominately white institutions (PWIs) that forcefully taught me how to shift, form, and adhere to whiteness. The most violent part of it was that, as a Black and Asian woman, my acceptance required recognizing the way I functioned in a white man's fantasy. I spoke, but not too much. I hunched my posture so I wouldn't take up space. If a man told me to wear less makeup or dress in a different style, I would do it. I convinced myself that my empowerment rested in their approval. I once had a white conservative Christian boyfriend who told me, "You're the perfect woman because you're sexy like a Black girl, subservient like an Asian girl, and you got that big black ass and that tight Asian pussy." I'm embarrassed to admit that when he said this, I believed I had achieved something in life.

I belittled the women who couldn't do what I was doing. I told myself that I was successful and better than them because I was palatable to the abusers. I, unfortunately, was Sarai.

The good news is that while the women of the Bible can't change their course of action, knowing their stories helps us to change ours. I was a Sarai because I thought appealing to powerful people would help me accept myself. The truth is that if I didn't accept myself to begin with, then these actions were nothing but vain attempts to solve a problem I didn't have the capacity to understand. Becoming palatable for white evangelical men doesn't solve their racism or sexism. I naively believed my body was the altar of repentance. I chose the role of bottom bitch over and over again because I didn't understand liberation. Choosing to be palatable meant that I denied myself the ability to feel my depression, despair, and rage. I chose to have an outward context of blissful ignorance while internally blaming myself for the violence of whiteness and patriarchy. In order to know liberation, I had to free myself from my desire to please the figures of power.

Power is narcissistic in function and character. This is not to say that every person pursuing power is a narcissist, which is an important distinction. I believe there are people who wholeheartedly want to expose and overthrow violent exploitive authority. That is a noble goal, but as the saying goes, "The road to hell is paved with good intentions." Good intentions can only get us so far, and vapid attempts to enact justice will be wasted. Too often I come across people who want to end the oppressive systems of anti-Blackness, racism, xenophobia, patriarchy, and cis-heteronormativity. However, their passion is not liberation for all people but rather an amplification of their own voice and opinions. When it comes to freeing people from the bondage of generational and institutional violence, exploitation and oppression, I now have little interest in entertaining someone else's vanity. Nor do I want to create space for clanging symbols that lack the depth to pursue a solidarity built on love.

When I embraced the divinity of Jesus, I had this belief that holiness meant conformity to whiteness and patriarchy. It took years for me to uproot that lie. As I deconstructed my internalized oppression, I found my voice and the desire to use it unapologetically. I stopped shrinking to assimilate to people, places, and dynamics that harmed me. It was a beautiful feeling to share my voice, but also worrisome because I had been socialized my entire life to center my abusers. Words like *disobedient* and *backsliding* were thrown around as attempts to retain control, but shrinking yourself is not the same as obedience to God, no matter what many of us are made to believe.

When I stopped shrinking, I began to connect with Hagar. She witnessed the violence Abram did to Sarai, and her body bore the swollen belly and the painful scars of Sarai's abuse. Sarai shrunk to fit into Abram's world, transferring the violence she received from her abuser onto someone she had power over. Hagar was a victim of this dynamic, but she did not submit to it. Most preaching I've heard on Hagar's story has told me that her shift occurs when she meets God at the well and names the deity *El-roi,* "the God who sees" (Gen. 16:13). I disagree. I think the shift happens earlier, when she flees Abram's dysfunctional household. Before she could know God as the one who sees her, Hagar had to be able to see herself as worthy enough to leave.

It's not easy to leave an abuser. We must unlearn the manipulations to which our minds succumbed. Many times that unlearning process means fighting back with defiance, grit, tears, and questioning one's sanity. Rather than simply walking away, leaving violence is a multistep process. It is not completed just by removing one's body. To truly leave places of violence, we must undo all the ways we were made to believe our dependence and blind devotion to it were necessary. In working with women fleeing domestic violence, I have found that the struggle is not getting a woman to leave a violent partner. The struggle is helping her believe she is worthy enough to escape. The same struggle existed within my story: to leave white evangelicalism, I had to believe that God's love for me was bigger than the idea that holiness meant assimilation to whiteness. Violence—whether it is interpersonal, intrapersonal, or institutional—will shape our minds to normalize abuse and blind us from knowing that we deserve to be treated differently.

Escaping violence involves uprooting lies and casting off blame so that we can wholeheartedly say, "I do not deserve this." The ability to even utter that sentence is a triumph. The ability to sustain that belief is a transformative prayer that requires us to embrace our despair and our rage to create the pathway that moves us to liberation. I used to be petrified of my rage. Growing up in violence will either teach you how to emulate violence or how to fold and shrink yourself to appease the abuser. I believed that the latter decision was safest, so I objectified myself by not allowing myself to experience despair, sadness, or rage. Instead, I directed those emotions toward myself and created blame scripts that kept me in a state of perpetual woundedness and hindered me from leaving. When I see Hagar, I see a woman who never denies her emotional range. She embraces her sadness and her rage so that she can flee her abusers. To be Hagar is to see the violence that silences, suppresses, and assaults us, to look it directly in the eye, and to say, "I don't deserve this."

It's important to acknowledge that Hagar chose her safety before she interacted with the Lord. She could not have met with the angel of the Lord at the spring in the desert if she had not fled. And what the Lord required of her next would not have been possible if she had not held tight to her truth. God said, "Return to your mistress, and submit to her" (Gen. 16:9–10).

I'll be honest, this is a part in the story where I say a lot of four-letter words. God told Hagar to go back to the person who's hurting her? And to *submit*? WHY? HOW? That's not OK to me. But I was taught to obey this story and to pledge absolute allegiance to it. Once womanism was introduced into my life, I had the space to question it and walk away from it altogether. I was able to tell God that I had questions about this and that I wanted my questions to give me more questions and better findings.

Too often we hear this verse telling us to return to the place of harm, violence, and enslavement. As both a lover of Scripture and the descendant of enslaved Africans and colonized Filipinx peoples, I simply cannot believe that those interpretations are valid. I hold tightly to the descriptions of God's kingdom as the place where weapons of war are turned into tools for cultivation (Isa. 2:1–4), where the sounds of weeping and the cries of distress will no longer exist

(65:19–20), and where normalized systems of violence and death will pass away (Rev. 21:4). I cannot believe the Lord would tell Hagar to return to the place where she would become victim again to the violence she had fled. So then what *does* it mean to return to the place of harm?

While I don't believe it is a good idea to return to a violent place, I also know that there are certain situations in which returning is inevitable. Whether it's returning briefly to a dysfunctional family system, an unhealthy community, or coparenting with an unhealthy ex-partner, there are circumstances when returning can be necessary. I don't recommend this path for everyone, nor do I want to interrupt their holy act of consent. What I do know is that returning to a place or people does not mean you succumb to the environment and become the victim again. Healing is a part of the returning.

Hagar realized that she did not deserve Abram's and Sarai's abuse. She fled because she knew her worth. When the angel of the Lord told her to return, he did not say, "You must return to Abram and Sarai because you're not valuable to God." Rather, God affirmed the worthiness that Hagar recognized in herself and promised her that, like Abram, she would be the progenitor of a great multitude (Gen. 16:10). It is because Hagar had the strength to reclaim and proclaim her personhood that God entrusted her with the task of returning.

What I find so tricky about this verse is how the angel of the Lord communicates what she must do: "Return to your mistress and submit to her." The word *submit* is the problem. I know my ancestors' history of being kidnapped, enslaved, trafficked, and colonized, as well as my personal experience growing up in a system of domestic violence, racism, and misogyny. Interwoven with my story and the story of my people is violence, pain, desperation, anxiety, depression, and hopelessness. Lashings and beatings, assault and rape, violence and exploitation—these experiences are markings within my family's story. Despite it all, I exist, but how do I celebrate this existence knowing that, like Hagar, my ancestors survived by submitting to such cruelty?

Here's the thing: submission does not mean assimilation, accepting the power structure of the culture and becoming blindly obedient to it. In celebrating the Lord as El-roi, "the God who sees" (Gen.

16:13), Hagar made a statement of defiance against the systems that sought to suppress her identity and erase her personal agency. It is true that she returned to Abram and Sarai, but she did not return the same person. She fled as an enslaved woman who was impregnated by her enslaver. She returned as someone seen, validated, and equipped by the God of her abusers. She returned knowing that she would become the mother of a nation. Enslaved, impoverished, impregnated, and forcibly displaced, she did not wield the power to overthrow Abram's tribe, but she did have a promise that ensured her survival within that violent dynamic. Hagar's liberation depended on her clinging to a promise that extended beyond her death. In the throes of violence, abuse, and manipulation, it is the promise that will sustain us. For many people, clinging to a promise was the only thing they had to combat gaslighting and live assuredly in their truth. Hagar's return models the power of knowing your truth, claiming your worth, and using a promise to reject a system of violence. Hagar submitted to Abram and Sarai, but she didn't assimilate to their abusive culture.

When taking a wide view of the overall story of liberation from sin, we must hold two truths in our hearts:

1. To become liberated peoples who dismantle and destroy systems of oppression, we must recognize that we exist within an intergenerational effort. In other words, the movement began before you, and it will continue after you.
2. Whatever marking of freedom we hold today exists because someone defied authority and chose not to assimilate or blindly follow a system of oppression.

I come from people who were stuck under systems of terrorism created by colonization, imperialism, and enslavement. I also come from people who didn't give themselves fully to the cultures that dehumanized them. There are small pieces of ourselves, our cultures, and our ways of knowing the world before colonization that remain intact as we search for other fragmented shards of who we are.

I realize that my own strength was made possible by my ancestors' efforts to see, hold, and advocate for their humanity. I am shaped by their prayers and formed by their resilience. Like Hagar, they called the Creator by the name El-roi and did not assimilate to the culture that dehumanized them. When you are seen, humanized, affirmed, and known by God, your liberation is implanted within your healing. You uproot lies. You unlearn violence. You're not the bottom bitch; you are the one liberated from that system of dysfunction.

In 2018 I became an on-site mentor in a home for women who had aged out of the foster care system. They were part of an invisible and highly underserved community known as "transition-age foster youth" (TAY). These women had experienced different forms of insufferable violence that had placed them in the foster care system. Before taking on this role, I was trained by experts in social work, psychology, and trauma-informed care. Throughout the training, one message came through clearly: at some point the TAY will return to their family of origin. That was the most painful truth I held as their mentor: there are situations in which returning to the place of harm is inevitable. My role was to provide support instead of enforcing control. There were many cases when this happened. During those times my heart broke, my worries deepened, and my body felt heavy from the anxieties I held. But I knew that it wasn't my job to control their story.

I also learned in the TAY training that returning to a place of harm can be a sign of success, not failure. A marker of this success is developing relationships that help abuse survivors understand what type of treatment they deserve so they have the tools to advocate for what they need when they return to relationships where harm happened. We can call these "restorative relationships." A restorative relationship helps people redefine what type of treatment will become their new normal. Harm caused in an abusive relationship can be healed in a restorative relationship. Healed persons will reenter the place of harm with a set of tools to protect themselves and advocate for their humanity.

Toxic people unravel when they encounter a person who is healing. Unhealthy people will mock boundaries, scoff at healing practices, and try to challenge the ways their former victims advocate for themselves. Eventually a healed person who is unwilling to compromise to a culture of violence will be exiled. The ultimatum is simple: you can either assimilate to this culture of violence, or you can leave. A similar situation happened between Sarai and Hagar:

> But Sarah saw the son of Hagar the Egyptian, whom she had borne to Abraham, playing with her son Isaac. So she said to Abraham, "Cast out this slave woman with her son, for the son of this slave woman shall not inherit along with my son Isaac." (Gen. 21:9–10)

This scene takes place years after Hagar's first encounter with the angel of the Lord. She returned to her mistress, remained enslaved, and survived whatever treatment Sarai gave her. Her son, Ishmael, became a cherished son of Abraham. Though little is said of Hagar in this scene, we can see that her child knows joy and is able to laugh freely. It is his laughter that unravels Sarah. Sarah's violence could not destroy Hagar because Hagar did not assimilate to the culture of violence. She maintained an unshakeable joy that she passed down to Ishmael. I imagine that the sound of Ishmael's laughter was like a ringing in Sarah's ears. To Sarah, the sound of Ishmael's joy symbolized Hagar's resistance.

Sarah's role was to uphold the system created to help Abraham achieve his goal of having a fruitful tribe, but Hagar's interaction with the angel of the Lord started an intervention that dismantled the culture of violence set by her enslavers. Sarah, who was both unhealed and unaware of her own toxicity, decided that the best strategy to protect the tribe was to forcibly exile the one who was disobedient.

Exile is a common strategy that a bottom bitch will use to protect the trafficker and keep those who are trafficked in line. While it is devastating to see Hagar and Ishmael forced into exile by the tribe of Abraham, we must also recognize that this is a victory. She's not in the place of harm. Hagar survived in that dysfunctional system for years. As she continued to heal and become a woman seen by God, she could not stay with her mistress. Sarah realized it, and—unbeknownst to her—she affirmed Hagar's need for liberation from the toxic system. The exile was an intervention.

There will come a time in your healing journey when you can no longer stay in the system that abused you. Sometimes you are the one who leaves; other times you are forced to leave. No matter how it happens, you are thrust into the wilderness. You may find yourself in a place of desperation like Hagar in Genesis 21:15–17:

> When the water in the skin was gone, she cast the child under one of the bushes. Then she went and sat down opposite him a good way off, about the distance of a bowshot, for she said, "Do not let me look on the death of the child." And as she sat opposite him, she lifted up her voice and wept. And God heard the voice of the boy, and the angel of God called to Hagar from heaven and said to her, "What troubles you, Hagar? Do not be afraid, for God has heard the voice of the boy where he is."

Leaving a toxic environment is not easy. You will find yourself alone, vulnerable, thirsty, and wondering if you'll survive the desolation. Hagar's position isn't romantic. She was on the edge of death. She was free and also very desperate. But she did not turn back. Instead of returning and begging to be accepted, instead of assimilating, Hagar stayed in the desert.

Here we find a stark difference between Sarah and Hagar: Sarah had power but was still enslaved, while Hagar had no power but was free.

Healing cannot happen in toxic places. Liberation is not won by appealing to power or upholding its standards. Narcissism is the primary function of power, and those who assimilate to its delusions already have sacrificed their humanity to maintain systems of violent dominance. They deny themselves the ability to acknowledge their despair, sadness, rage, or even the deep joy which are the human emotions that spark liberation. This is the unfortunate reality of the bottom bitches: they relinquish their agency and steadily feed themselves and others on a metaphorical diet of gaslighting in order to help the abusers achieve their goal.

Eventually Hagar had another wilderness encounter in which God met her in that time of desperation, provided her with water, and affirmed that Ishmael would not be abandoned. They did not return to the toxic place. In their healing they discovered that God sees, affirms, and provides. Their lives would no longer be defined by submission to a violent system that justified harm. They refused to please the privileged and perpetuate systems of power.

There were decades of my life when I was Sarah. I violently abused myself and gaslit others in order to create a false sense of safety that I thought would sustain me. Every day that I was the bottom bitch was another day of death. In the white evangelical church I often heard people rephrase the words of Christ and tell me that I needed to die to myself. What they meant was that they needed my rage, Blackness, Asianness, and womanness to die. They needed me to die so that they could feel comfortable. I was made to believe that holiness was the act of steadily feeding myself on a diet of lies and self-hatred.

Now I exist in these years of being Hagar. I am a woman of color who can no longer stand to be an object for someone else's abuse. My rage no longer scares me because I know that it is the pathway to liberation. I thought self-acceptance was measured by how well I could assimilate into an environment that wanted to detach me from my identity, my cultures, and my ancestors. That wasn't self-acceptance; it was a form of internalized colonization. True self-acceptance is rooted in radical self-love. It doesn't seek the approval of my abusers, nor does it detach me from my identity.

I am learning to lead with a radical self-love that extends into community care. When Hagar did the radical act of naming God as El-Roi, she not only did it for herself but to proclaim it so that other victims of violence would know it deep within their bones and create revolutionary communities of healing people who are seen and known by God.

I still have that journal I wrote in when I was sixteen years old. Every so often I'll read it to remember how far I've come and to celebrate the ways I have been liberated. I look at the ways that girl held so much self-hatred and inflicted mental and physical torture on herself. I see the ways she tried, with every ounce of her being, to write herself to safety. The truth is that I could not have become the woman I am today until I took my Hagar journey and fled the house of the abuser.

Chapter Three

Leah and Dinah

When the LORD saw that Leah was unloved, he opened her womb, but Rachel was barren. Leah conceived and bore a son, and she named him Reuben, for she said, "Because the LORD has looked on my affliction, surely now my husband will love me." She conceived again and bore a son and said, "Because the LORD has heard that I am hated, he has given me this son also," and she named him Simeon. Again she conceived and bore a son and said, "Now this time my husband will be joined to me, because I have borne him three sons"; therefore he was named Levi. She conceived again and bore a son and said, "This time I will praise the LORD," therefore she named him Judah; then she ceased bearing.

—Gen. 29:31–35

When Shechem son of Hamor the Hivite, prince of the region, saw [Dinah], he seized her and lay with her by force. And his soul was drawn to Dinah daughter of Jacob; he loved the young woman and spoke tenderly to her.

—Gen. 34:2–3

All the Words We Couldn't Hear

(pick your apology or affirmation)

after Layli Long Soldier

my

mother   daughter

I am   we're still   I regret

holding   mourning   carrying   silencing

you   truth   sorrow   autonomy   ourselves

how I wish   dare I say   let me forget   help us release   do not hide   please release

your   my   our   their   his

truth   independence   choices   decisions

allow   stop   slow

the harm   the promises

to find us

Patriarchy

I'm fond of the word *gossip*.
The English word comes from "god-sib," like a godparent. This definition, rooted in Christianity, suggests meaningful conversation with a trusted relation rather than the murmurings of a facetious manipulator or sower of chaos. Because it is rooted in perception, gossip requires deep relationship and discernment. I can't share information with someone that I do not have a relationship with, but information sharing can be an opportunity to begin establishing relationship with a new person to discern their character, values, and level of safety.

Filipinx people are gossips. (I name this lovingly.) We have a term for our practice of frequent gossip: *tsismosa* culture. Our cultural value of kapwa promotes this deep inner and interrelational connection. Our evidence for it is made clear: the Philippines has the lowest rate of serial killers in the world. As one person on Reddit explained, "It's hard to be a serial killer in a country where everyone is so nosy and all up in your business."[1]

Filipinx people have two favorite pastimes: basketball and gossip. The former is a by-product of Western colonization and militarization within the nation built of more than 7,000 islands. The latter is a cultural value that creates a questionable system of safety for a people who live in an economically destabilized country, lost their ancestral ways by way of colonization (by the Japanese, Spain, and the United States), and are one of the first nations to feel the impact of climate change (not by their own fault, of course, but due to the irresponsibility of countries in the Global North). This is the hidden ethic of *tsismosa* culture: the use of gossip as a postcolonial tool to keep us safe.

In his book *Grooming, Gossip, and the Evolution of Language*, psychologist Robin Dunbar asserts that human language developed through our ability to pass on information in order to construct systems of social order and cohesion. This is in stark contrast to male-centered studies in anthropology, which claim that male-centered activities, like hunting, developed language for survival. While predatory animals certainly did pose an external threat, Dunbar states that the use of language as a means of harm reduction was centered on the internal threats that happened within human relationships. This study, known as the "gossip theory," revealed that humanity's quest to reduce harm and find flourishing depended on having reliable information to determine who was trustworthy, who needed help, and who was harmful to the group. As populations grew and more social groups formed, gossip continued to be the main tool for harm reduction, collective survival, and developing more sophisticated relationship structures.[2]

Gossip, at its core, is a form of truth telling.

What interests me about the use of the word *gossip* in Scripture is the timing of it. The King James Version of the Bible was published in 1611—years after the word *gossip* became synonymous with femininity and slander, women's idle chatter. In the original biblical languages, however, the Hebrew word *rakil* (as in Prov. 11:13 and 20:19) is a masculine word meaning "scandalmonger." The Greek word *psithyristas* (as in Rom. 1:29) is an accusatory masculine word used specifically to describe a slanderer who covertly destroys another person's character. Slander is rooted in lies. Gossip is rooted in truth telling and accountability. When people can speak plainly about the actions of an abusive or predatory person, they are not engaging in slander but advocacy. Gossip is not sin; it is the way we expose sinners in a world that provides so little retribution and accountability for the crimes done to us.

In our post-KJV world, accusations of gossip are misogynistically used to undermine and villainize our tools for safety. When I come across sermons and messages that say, "Don't be a gossip," what I am really hearing is, "Conform to our systems of power." I sneer when I read women's devotionals telling us not to be gossips. The irony of it makes my stomach churn; we are told not to engage in the activity that was born of our foremothers and is associated with keeping women safe. It feels like the authors are belittling what could have been the only tool available to protect their communities. Instead, I want to say this: slandering is a sin, but gossip can keep us protected.

When I think of gossip, I think of Leah and Dinah. One used gossip to her benefit, while the other suffered from not being heard. Leah was a matriarch who used gossip to maintain her family. Dinah was Leah's daughter who suffered from her father's silence and in being silenced within the narrative.

Jacob had four wives and thirteen kids. There was gossip. Jacob's role was to provide, protect, and maintain the family's abundance. He was the one who maintained the tribe's power and enlisted his sons to do the labor needed for the family to thrive. As the patriarch, Jacob established the systems of social control to maintain his reputation as a rich and powerful patriarch. As his first wife, Leah had the job of maintaining social order within their family and upholding Jacob's reputation among other tribes. Jacob had the power and control, while his first wife maintained his influence and respectability. Her power existed in the society-building tool associated with women: truth telling and information sharing. I imagine she maintained a keen ear over the gossip within her household, which consisted of a trickster husband, his three additional wives, and the thirteen kids of their tribe. Gossip is not a system of power; it is a system of safety for those who lack it.

When I read Leah's story, I consider all the ways that she has been a victim to patriarchy in her life: daughter to a manipulative father, wife to a righteous con man, and the forgotten matriarch of a tribe. Many interpretations of her story carry the same tone: "Isn't it so sad that Jacob loved Rachel more, but at least Leah is in Jesus' bloodline!" Even her "weak eyes" (as some translate Gen. 29:17) are subjugated to perpetuate this weird Christian patriarchal myth that God favors the modest.

What is not seen are the ways that Leah has survived under the immense amount pressed upon her. Leah is the only female character in the Bible whose story reflects two different generational burdens impressed on women. She is also saddled with the responsibility of maintaining the family's safety and survival. Leah is more than watery eyes and sucks-for-her biblical interpretations. She is the eldest daughter who eventually becomes the matriarch.

Knowing Leah deeply means we should first know her name. *Leah* means "cow." While that may be laughable to us now, it holds high significance for who she was and the time she lived in. Leah's father was a wealthy man with a lot of livestock, and he named his daughters to reflect this wealth. Laban named Rachel, Leah's younger sister and Jacob's favored wife, "ewe" or "sheep." On a personal level, I find these terms objectifying. I catch myself asking questions: Why would Laban name his daughters after animals? Were they nothing but livestock to him? Despite my frustrations, I am also reminded that these names reflect Laban's pride and potentially his affection toward his daughters. He is a man whose wealth exists because of his livestock, and naming his daughters "cow" and "ewe" also meant they were valuable to him. There's another dimension to Leah's name: the meaning of her name, cow, reflects Nanna, a Mesopotamian goddess associated with cowherds, the menstrual cycle, and fertility. Leah is known by the wealth she brings as a herder and the abundance she brings with childbearing.

When I think of Leah, I think of my friends who are the oldest daughters of their immigrant families. They have a high sense of obligation. They are assistants to parents navigating a new society and unofficial mothers to siblings more acquainted with this new land. They are taking care of everyone's needs while miraculously remaining uncrushed by high expectations. The same is true of Leah. I see it in the way Laban swapped Rachel for Leah during Jacob and Rachel's wedding night. Jacob thought he was going to have sex with his bride and instead took Leah. I read these passages with one part outrage and another part understanding. My outrage says, "Wow, Laban, you're a greedy jerk who just loves to ruin people's lives." After all, Laban knew Jacob's love for Rachel made him gullible to manipulation. Laban pulling this dirty move got Jacob to add seven more years of servitude to him. My understanding, created in part by being the daughter of an immigrant family, sees Laban as a man who is doing what he can to maintain generational wealth. He knows he will lose a large portion of his wealth once his daughters are married, so he is doing what he can to ensure the wealth isn't squandered. Leah and Rachel were herders who knew how to take care of livestock. Up until this point, Jacob was known as a trickster who stole his brother's blessing and ran away from home.

As the daughter of an immigrant, I had to learn that there are differences between violence and doing what needs to be done to ensure survival. Living in a power-based society that lacks resources and support for vulnerable families is the true violence.

Leah is continuously put in vulnerable positions and, at every turn, proves her cunning and usefulness. She has survived living with a father who objectifies her and a husband who does not love her. She has helped both men gain abundance. Her story fits her name: she brings fertility and wealth to her household. There is a moment when we see this happen in Genesis 30. Reuben, Leah's son, finds mandrakes in the field and brings them to his mother. Their special scent was considered an aphrodisiac, amplifying sexuality and purportedly bringing fertility and power to a person.[3] In this story, we find gossip at work. Reuben brings the mandrakes to his mother; Rachel, wanting to get pregnant, asks Leah to give the mandrakes to her. Leah responds to her sister plainly, "Is it a small matter that you have taken away my husband? Would you take away my son's mandrakes also?" (30:15). There is a part of me that reads this moment as a petty clapback made by a wounded Leah, but I think that interpretation flattens her character. Leah uses this line to invite Rachel into bartering with her, and Rachel heeds. Rachel offers to trade her upcoming time with Jacob for the mandrakes. Both women get what they want: Leah gets Jacob's affection and bears him another son; Rachel gets the herbal medicine used to heal a barren womb. Their bartering is also how gossip works; the women are using their resourcefulness to improve their lives in a patriarchal society.

Before I continue, let me first explain what patriarchy is and isn't. The popular definition of patriarchy is that men are in charge. I have been a part of feminist circles that chanted, "Down with patriarchy," and mobilized strategies to shame men without understanding how they, too, have suffered in its violence. After a while, those methods grew stale because I found myself living to criticize and powermonger instead of moving to rebuild care-based communities and cultures that center liberation. bell hooks's book *The Will to Change: Men, Masculinity, and Love* shifted my understanding of patriarchy. In her words, "Patriarchy is a political-social system that insists that males are inherently dominating, superior to everything and everyone deemed weak, especially females, and endowed with the right to dominate and rule over the weak and to maintain that dominance through various forms of psychological terrorism and violence."[4]

To its core, patriarchy is rooted in the uneven allocation of power, moralizing what is superior and naming everything under it as weak. It needs suppression and violence in order to exist. It lives in how we are conditioned to suppress our emotions and never claim the truth of our belovedness and deservingness of safety and flourishing. It creates a dominator model of leadership that upholds violence and favors, if not normalizes, relationships as power struggles instead of places of shared intimacy. To liberate one person from the harm caused by patriarchy is to liberate us all to find a new way. I speak of patriarchy because the stories of Jacob and Leah give us a wide view of the pain patriarchy leaves behind.

Laban is the first generation. His determination to enforce obligation on Leah, marrying her covertly to a man who didn't want her, was a glimpse of how patriarchy disrupts familial bonds.

The second generation is Jacob and his many wives. Jacob spoke openly of his deep love for Rachel, leaving Leah knowing that she was unloved. Leah carried the weight of obligation as the eldest daughter of a migrant family and matriarch of Jacob's tribe. Their relationship was defined by domination and objectification.

The pain of the third generation is found in Dinah, a violence survivor whose pain was silenced. She didn't get a say in her own restoration.

Dinah is Leah's youngest child and Jacob's only daughter. Her name means "her judgment." It's unclear why Leah gave her this name. I choose to believe it's because Leah wanted Dinah to be able to have autonomy and trust her own judgment rather than the obligations forced upon her as a woman.

When Dinah is a young woman, she travels to see the daughters of the land and to gossip with them. Her journey is interrupted by a Hivite prince named Shechem who captures and rapes her. *Biastophilia* is a term that means one's sexual arousal is dependent on feeling power over an unconsenting stranger, and it refers to how people can mistake lust for power. Rape is about power, not sex or affection. This is what happens between Dinah and her rapist: he takes advantage of her, then shows deep affection for her and seeks to make her his bride. Scripture describes Shechem's affection as his soul being drawn to Dinah's. Rather than being romantic, however, this shows me that he values and benefits from a culture that normalizes violence and dominance as the hallmarks of relationship.

Scripture states that Jacob learns of what happened to Dinah before Shechem and his father, Hamor, arrive to announce their intention for marriage. Jacob holds that gossip to himself as Hamor speaks with Jacob, which just so happens to be the moment when Jacob's sons arrive and hear what happened. The sons are indignant and yell accusations at Hamor while Hamor is offering a deal to have their families intermarry and cohabitate. The sons are enraged about Dinah's rape; Hamor is presenting it as a good business deal. Jacob remains silent. And Shechem makes his final plea: "Let me find favor with you, and whatever you say to me I will give. Put the marriage present and gift as high as you like, and I will give whatever you ask me; only give me the young woman to be my wife" (Gen. 34:11–12).

But where is Dinah? She is not where the yelling and negotiations happen, nor is she present when Jacob and his sons come to a compromise with Shechem and Hamor (which turns out to be a trick). I choose to believe Dinah is in the place where patriarchy cannot reach. She is seeking a tenderness that will calm a body and soul that were overpowered by domination. I want to believe Dinah is with her mother, weeping in her arms and begging her to go back in time. Leah, who understands what it is like to be objectified and have her body used in unconsented marriages made to perpetuate male dominance, is holding her close and wiping her tears. Then Rachel, Zilpah, and Bilhah enter, running to Dinah and holding her close. This is a moment in the shadow of Scripture where a daughter and her many mothers offer each other truth telling and tenderness in the security of their own tent.

This is gossip too.

In the end, Leah and Dinah cannot escape patriarchy. They use gossip as a tool to strengthen their relationships and stay connected to each other, but they cannot get free. It is difficult for me to read this story and not end up hopeless as I dream of a world without patriarchy. I must remember that healing in a system that tries to control and dominate you is still a victory. The ways we survive deserve as much honor as the ways we dismantle and rebuild.

This is a book about healing as much as it is about liberation. But if liberation is ultimately what we seek, do we continue our acts of healing in hopes that they develop a snowball effect that leads us toward a new reality? I like the idea of it, but I know it's not enough. We must walk with intentionality.

Gossip is a form of resistance creating an ethic of safety within a community that is marginalized and has experienced harm. It's associated with women because it's born of women-centered communities. When I think of dismantling patriarchy and its systems of dominance, I must look to the ways communities exist without patriarchy. I must look at matriarchies. The first thing to understand about matriarchy is that it's not about role reversal, but about a radical reordering of the way society operates.

Heidi Goettner-Abendroth, a cultural anthropologist, feminist scholar, and founder of the International Academy for Modern Matriarchal Studies and Matriarchal Spirituality, defines matriarchies as "non-hierarchal, horizontal societies of matrilineal kinship."[5] Her research and observation of contemporary matriarchies, which are most often Indigenous agricultural societies, led her to define matriarchies using four levels of criteria: economics, social patterns, political decision making, and cultural foundations.

- At the economic level, matriarchal economies distribute goods across kinship lines or within families. A kinship line or family can be either biological or chosen family, depending on the cultural context of the group. A matriarchy is rooted in a "gift economy," which gives gifts to satisfy needs and validate the humanity of the one receiving the gift. The economic goal of a matriarchy is to develop communal balance. As Indigenous botanist Robin Wall Kimmerer explains in her book *Braiding Sweetgrass*, "In the gift economy, gifts are not free. The essence of the gift is that it creates a set of relationships. The currency of a gift economy is, at its root, reciprocity."[6]
- In a matriarchy, social patterns are determined by the mother's

line and created through marriages between extended clans. Kinship determines social position, political titles, and allocation of goods in the gift economy. Family is at the center of the social pattern, with one household "hold[ing] anywhere from ten to more than one hundred persons depending on size and architectural style."[7] Even though women hold the power of distribution, matriarchal societies do not have a ruling class, underresourced or underserved peoples, or systems of domination.

• Political decision making in a matriarchy is all-inclusive. As Goettner-Abendroth explains, "After thorough discussion, each decision is taken by consensus. The same is true for the entire village: if matters concerning the whole village have to be discussed, delegates from every clan-house meet in the village council."[8] Political decisions are determined by the whole village.

• The cultural foundations of a matriarchy are rooted in a spirituality in which people and nature are interconnected. There is no secular or religious separation; everything is holy and has a divinity worth protecting.

I'm aware that I sound crazy in proposing we migrate toward developing a matriarchal society. (I relinquished the idea of being sane and assimilated a long time ago.) Some level of craziness is important when pursuing the abolitionist reality that is God's kingdom. I've often wondered if pursuing this path would be heretical, but when I see the harm found within the stories of Leah and Dinah, I realize that I really don't care about what is considered heretical. I care about restoration and flourishing, because that's what Jesus' life reflected. The very life, death, and resurrection of Jesus is God's way of implementing a gift economy rooted in grace and valuing our humanity over our sinfulness (Eph. 2:10). He educated his community of followers and disciples to rebuke social hierarchies (John 13:16). Jesus' brother, James, taught us that developing a praxis reflecting God's kingdom begins with how we listen to one another (Jas. 1:19). Instead of separating humanity from nature, Jesus explains that if humanity is silent then we will hear the rocks cry out to the Creator (Luke 19:40).

There is much to say about dismantling the patriarchy in favor of an equitable system built on valuing humanity over power. Studies and research are important, but they shouldn't negate our movement toward action and development. Dismantling and deconstruction have an important role in liberation, but all too often I find that it is an intellectual pursuit instead of a lived reality. How disappointing it is to see people talk of freedom and allow Leah's and Dinah's narratives of silence and suffering to be perpetuated in our everyday lives.

It was the Black women in my life who helped me believe that matriarchy can exist beautifully and well within our urban contexts: the consistent and steady love of my Aunt Estine, my Aunt Gloria's determination to know our ancestors' stories, the organizing of historical and contemporary abolitionists. It is in the genius of Black female writings from bell hooks, June Jordan, Toni Morrison, Angela Davis, and Audre Lorde. They remind me that living in a patriarchal society does not mean that I must submit to its confines. We can reclaim our ancestral heritage and build new worlds as the current one tries to kill us.

Precolonial West African tribes were built of matrilineal societies that developed their communities through the mother's bloodline. When colonial enslavers tortured and kidnapped our Indigenous African ancestors, they centered their violence on emasculating Black men, adultifying Black children, oversexualizing Black childless women, and asexualizing Black mothers. That final tactic was practiced by violently forcing Black mothers to neglect their biological children in order to care for their enslavers' children. From this form of torture and familial separation came the Mammy stereotype: a Black woman who tended to the needs of others, brought communal wisdom, and wasn't interested in her own needs. The Mammy stereotype is a hindrance to recognizing the genius of Black matriarchy. In order to fully (and monetarily) celebrate and honor the Black matriarch, one must deconstruct and reject all the ways one has been indoctrinated to objectify Black women.

In her book *When Momma Speaks: The Bible and Motherhood from a Womanist Perspective*, Stephanie Buckhanon Crowder breaks down the different ways Black matriarchy appears as a form of resistance to anti-Blackness and patriarchy.[9] Biological mothers—whether single or married—are forced to be strong for their families to survive in

America's violently oppressive societies. Institutional racism, economic disparities, and incarceration target Black men in order to uphold systems of enslavement that propel American free market economics. Thus, the biological Black matriarchs resort to what is necessary to keep the family unit together. When parental figures are absent (by way of force or choice), the role of Black matriarch goes to the grandmother, tasked to care for the children so they do not go into the foster care system, which is rife with its own traumatic experiences. The Black matriarch does what she is able to do in order to prevent children from becoming prey to the foster-care-to-prison pipeline.

Black matriarchy also exists outside of the family unit; we see it in our churches and on the streets. A Black church mother is the one who breathes life into the vision of the church community. The church mother's leadership goes beyond the roles of making meals, attending Bible studies, and mobilizing the women of the church for special events. She plays an important role in determining how Black women can heal in these spiritual communities. This role, of course, is dependent on the health of the church mother herself. I have seen Black church mothers uplift Black and non-Black women of color to expand beyond the repressive boxes whiteness and patriarchy give us. At other times I have seen church mothers who lead from their own unhealed bitterness, participating in women being confined to roles that cause harm and encouraging them to "wait out" abuse.

The final iteration of the Black matriarch is the community mother. The community mother is the one who actively defies the systems of oppression that hinder our collective flourishing. She does so through advocacy, education, community organizing, and protest. While there are many Black women activists and organizers, the community mother is dedicated to organizing at the grassroots level to cast vision and develop the next generation of empire dismantlers. In every point of the history of the United States you will find a community mother seeking liberation for all. Some of my favorite historical community mothers include Mary MacLeod Bethune, Fannie Lou Hamer, Marsha P. Johnson, and Stacey Abrams.

What I love about Black matriarchy in our contemporary Western contexts is that it gives us the framework for understanding how to subvert and dismantle the systems that bind us. We are still learning and building our paths toward collective liberation—always learning from those who came before us. There are people who would argue against me and say that Black matriarchy is not perfect, that it is too flawed, or that Black women are insufficient leaders. These are people so deeply rooted in patriarchy that they cannot see the misogynoir that seeps from their polluted and porous psyches. There are also people who seek to co-opt the organizing brilliance of Black women. They are parasites who devour the nutrients of our movements toward collective flourishing. There are people who scoff and say this is unbiblical, but I have yet to see patriarchy and power-based ministries serve a morsel of heaven. The kingdom of God is the place rooted in the equitable nourishment of the *imago Dei*. It is the place where people are safe, their voices are known, their needs are met, and the gift economy aids our collective flourishing. A matriarchy isn't about women having power; it's about people subverting power so that we can thrive in communities that cherish and nourish every expression of our personhood.

Chapter Four

Potiphar's Wife

Now Joseph was handsome and good-looking. And after a time his master's wife cast her eyes on Joseph and said, "Lie with me." But he refused and said to his master's wife, "Look, with me here, my master has no concern about anything in the house, and he has put everything that he has in my hand. He is not greater in this house than I am, nor has he kept back anything from me except yourself, because you are his wife. How then could I do this great wickedness and sin against God?" And although she spoke to Joseph day after day, he would not consent to lie beside her or to be with her. One day, however, when he went into the house to do his work, and while no one else was in the house, she caught hold of his garment, saying, "Lie with me!" But he left his garment in her hand and fled and ran outside. When she saw that he had left his garment in her hand and had fled outside, she called out to the members of her household and said to them, "See, my husband has brought among us a Hebrew to insult us! He came in to me to lie with me, and I cried out with a loud voice, and when he heard me raise my voice and cry out, he left his garment beside me and fled outside."

—Gen. 39:6–15

I

Watch the night. Fold over us. We pray dreams. Birth and abundance. The Goddess Nut. Daughter of fertility. She births moons. Over and over. Teach me how. Bless my womb. For Egypt's sake. Every full moon. We dance prayers. Every new moon. I cry terror. Barren military wife. Threat to empire. This is duty. Birth warring sons. To warring husband. Our warring family. Barren burden bad. I am she. Emptiness begs filling. Unpregnant still praying. Disappointing empire everymoon. This is exhausting. Priestess prophesied plans. Potiphar's seed unroots. Choose someone else. A gangly thing. Our enslaved one. He fascinates me. Loving our household. Is loving me. Sleep with me. No. Lie with me. No. Offer myself daily. No.

II

"Look, with me here, my master has no concern about anything in the house, and he has put everything that he has in my hand. He is not greater in this house than I am, nor has he kept back anything from me except yourself, because you are his wife. How then could I do this great wickedness and sin against God?"

III

I need sons. I need sons. I need sons. Lie with me. No. I'll make him. For Egypt's greatness. For Potiphar's glory. For my security. Lie with me. Or you'll suffer. As I have. Missed your chance. Give me evidence. Cloak now mine. Trophy for failing. Go to prison. For your treason. In denying me. Joseph failed Egypt. Treasonous. Treacherous. Tragic. My mission failed. Producing new mission. Choose another slave. Egypt must prevail. Womb a weapon. For empire's glory.

IV

My darling Potiphar. Caressing rounded betrayal. Done for Egypt. We are pregnant. Potiphar and I. Unknown birth father. Betrayal's not treason. Done for Egypt. Thank you, goddess. Birth like Nut.

Sons and moons. We'll make plenty. Watch the night. Fold over us. Ready to birth. Contractions ripping me. Midwives singing prayers. Birth chamber joy. Egypt's beloved baby. Ready to crown. Born into victory. Joy is palpable. Breath is waning. Something is happening. The singing stopped. Laughter to heaving. Now spinning voices. *A complication m'lady. Must calm down.* Body starts shaking. Hands on limbs. Is birthing cold? *Quickly. Quickly.* Footsteps are scurrying. *Bring in priestess. Don't fall asleep.* Closed my eyes. Woke to darkness. Death crowned baby. Everything was correct. Done for Egypt. How this ends. Breaks my soul. No more Nut. Begging new gods. Thoth and Anubis. Weigh my life. Let Osiris know. I was righteous. Please save us. Holding my prize. Wiping dry tears. A darling baby. For Egypt's greatness. Born into death. Mommy is here. Crying beside you. No one remembers. Names of women. Sacrificed for empires.

Purity Culture

If I must sit through another sermon in which a male pastor com-
pares himself to Joseph fleeing the temptation of Potiphar's wife, I
will climb over pews, rush the pulpit, and perform an exorcism.

Throughout my Christian life I have sat through eight (maybe
nine?) sermons in which a pastor will claim that Potiphar's wife was
something of an evil-sex-wildebeest-temptress sent by the devil. He
will talk of how he (or a friend of his) met one such temptress and,
like Joseph, ran away. Christians, being the incredibly horny people
that they are, cling to this story when they talk of righteousness and
sexual purity. All the while, they completely disregard how this story
is about the dynamics of how improper use of power and privilege
creates an atmosphere that justifies sexual violence. This misinterpretation ironically results in the same situation they preach of—a
disordered power dynamic. These pastors are not Joseph; they are
Potiphar's wife, forcing themselves on innocent victims and believing
their actions godly.

The purpose of this chapter is to explain how purity culture is
a pipeline to rape culture. Purity culture is a category of evangelical teaching that measures righteousness solely on sexual behavior,
and primarily operates by shaming women into chastity and shaming queer peoples into becoming heterosexual. As we'll see, this is
less about the pursuit of righteousness and more about the pursuit
of control. Rape, too, is about power and control; it's not about sex.
Rape utilizes nonconsensual or coerced sex to establish or maintain a
system of dominance that seeks to control another person or a group
of peoples. When Potiphar's wife used her power and privilege to
attempt to take advantage of Joseph, she became an attempted rapist. When the church uses coercion and sexual suppression to encourage disembodiment, transactional relationships, and self-denial, it
becomes an architect of rape culture.

I'm interested in Potiphar's wife because I know nearly nothing about
her. She is known for being a nameless temptress, a woman with a
wicked agenda to make pious men weak. She is slut-shamed throughout history. Potiphar's wife is used as an example to claim that bored

women will choose sex as their distraction of choice. With that thinking, the ultimatum given to Christian women is to avoid Potiphar's
wife's fate by keeping women occupied with patriarchal piety and
shamed into submission. She becomes nameless and shamed. It is
a similar practice forced upon my sisters and the queer and trans
siblings whom Christianity seeks to control and silence. We are slut-
shamed and made examples of. Our names are forgotten, and we
become sacrifices made to a religious and political agenda.

We must name her if we are to honor her. In the Qur'an, Potiphar's
wife is named Zuleikha. She is the wife of the captain of Egypt's military. In the Hebrew Bible, Potiphar is described as a *saris*, which translates as both "eunuch" and "court official." There is a level of mystery
here: Does this mean Potiphar is a eunuch? Or is he a court official? Is
it one, or is it both? Either way, both positions speak toward Zuleikha's
circumstances. If he is a eunuch, then their sex life is impacted. In
the Talmud there are certain contexts where *eunuch* refers to a person
who was intentionally castrated, and others where a condition more
closely aligned to sterility is implied. If he isn't a eunuch but instead
a military officer, then her role as his wife becomes a symbolic one in
Egypt's high court. Her husband, whose position is better translated
as "chief of the slaughterers," has an obligation to produce an heir to
symbolically prove the future of Egypt's stability and prosperity. I read
the story of her failed attempt at seduction with new eyes. Yes, she is
attracted to Joseph. She is also pressured to produce what her husband
can't or won't provide: an heir.

It is with the expectation of a nation on her shoulders and the
weight of an empty womb in her body that Zuleikha pursues Joseph.
She looks at Joseph with sultry eyes and desperation, repeatedly
inviting him into her bed. "Lie with me," she says, with her seduction and obligation. This is called quid pro quo sexual harassment,
when a person who is in a position of power seeks sexual favors from
a subordinate, offering some sort of benefit in return. When Joseph
refuses, she treats it as a denial of herself and her country. Scripture
states that Zuleikha tells him day after day to lie with her, and each
time he denies her. Finally, there is no one in the house to witness
or empathize with Joseph. She takes the opportunity, and he, once
again, denies her. This time he leaves behind his garment, however,

providing Zuleikha with evidence to shame and imprison him. Joseph is the survivor of repetitive sexual harassment and is punished for his refusal. To Zuleikha, it is more important for the country to thrive by any means necessary, which includes shaming and villainizing those who seek to protect themselves and their autonomy.

There is a misunderstanding about rape. A popular myth is that in order for rape to happen, the act has to be completed. That's a lie. Sexual harassment is a part of sexual violence. Rape culture is a setting that allows sexual violence to be normalized. Zuleikha constantly commanding Joseph to sleep with her is a form of sexual violence that Joseph endures. If Joseph had decided to give in to her commands, he would still be a rape victim. When sexual harassment is normalized, it perpetuates rape culture. Rape culture creates an environment where victims are degraded, living in fear, and forced to restrict their actions and behaviors. I see purity culture in the same vein: people are degraded into their "lock and key"* roles, afflicted with complex sexual trauma forming a constant state of fear surrounding sex, and indoctrinated to stop any exploration of their sexuality.[1] It is just as pervasive because it relies on sexual suppression and sexual harassment to pressure people with an agenda of holiness while also turning vulnerable populations—youth, women, disabled people, the LGBT+ community, and Black and non-Black people of color—into prey.

My own experiences with purity culture are mainly tied to my time in white evangelicalism and the Black Baptist church. The messaging was clear and consistent: our bodies are bad, extramarital sex is sinful, and women are at fault for tempting men. I was a student of these teachings and eventually spent years as a youth leader who impressed these same lessons on junior high and high schoolers. I spent years of my life immersed in purity pledges, celebrating purity rings, hearing of purity balls, creating "future husband" vision boards, listening to other women's "sextimonies" (testimonies of healing from sexual

---

*If you haven't heard of the lock and key metaphor, then you are truly blessed. It goes like this: Men are like keys (because they have a penis) and women are like locks (because of vaginas). A lock that can be opened by many keys isn't worth anything.

impurity), sharing my own sextimony, making "no more masturba-tion" vows, praying to be a young bride, praying for friends to find their spouse, and regurgitating statements like, "You should break up if you don't intend on getting married." All of it was very toxic, and we didn't question it because purity culture targeted us during a key period in our brain development.

While both spiritual spaces I inhabited spread the same message of purity culture, I recognize that their underlying motivations were very different. I believe these different motivations create separate contexts for how and why the spiritually abusive theology of purity culture allowed a generation of Christians to develop in an atmo-sphere where sexual violence and rape culture would permeate. For me to paint this picture, I'll need to share some of my own story.

My childhood was spent in consistently violent spaces. I was unsafe in my home, at school, and in the various sports activities that I participated in. Additionally, I was forming my identity as a Black and Asian woman in spaces dominated by whiteness, anti-Blackness, misogyny, xenophobia, and classism. All I knew was survival mode. The only way I knew how to cope with violence was through blam-ing myself rather than feeling the inevitable sting of retaliation from another person. I made self-shame and self-rejection my daily prac-tice so that I would not feel that pain from others. I took responsibil-ity for situations I had no part in, apologized frequently, and told myself that this hurt I inflicted on myself was better than the hurt I would receive from others. I believed that to be loved I had to be lov-able and in order to be respected I had to fit into others' standards of respectability. I entrusted my whole identity and worth to other peo-ple because it was unfathomable for me to believe that I could love myself. Perfectionism became the truth of my life; receiving the love and acceptance that I deserved meant I had to be impressive enough to earn it. Long before I stepped foot in a church, I was already well versed in the ways of self-hatred. Adopting purity culture into my personal ethic was easy.

Purity culture is a curriculum rooted in forming the mind of those who aren't cisgender men to embrace the pursuit of holiness through self-loathing. It is a shame story that parades itself as a fairy tale in which playing our part correctly will produce the Prince Charming who will provide us with the Christlike love we can only receive in heterosexual marriage. It presents disassociation as piety in order to develop a power dynamic that perpetuates silence, denies the practice of consent, and allows vulnerable people to fall victim to quid pro quo sexual harassment, sexual assault, and rape. This creates a breeding ground for pedophilia and makes sexual assault permissible. Intimacy becomes transactional, and affection is something that is consumed instead of shared. Young women are taught that our singular pursuit is to be a profitable transaction with a high return on investment. The return on investment is measured in four ways: our youthfulness, our ability to please our husbands, our ability to expand our family (biologically or through adoption), and our ability to perpetuate the relevance of what amounts to a sexual version of the prosperity gospel. The term "sexual prosperity gospel," created by journalist Katelyn Beaty, applies this crooked theology to sex by proclaiming that premarital abstinence will be rewarded with a good spouse, a healthy Christian marriage, great sex, and financial security. As Beaty explains, "Like all powerful myths, it offers the illusion of control in an unpredictable world. We are most tempted to adopt prosperity teachings for our greatest areas of vulnerability. This is why health and wealth teachings typically attract the financially struggling, and why the promise of sexual and marital fulfillment attracted so many sexually frustrated Christian teenagers."[2]

I was *definitely* one of those sexually frustrated Christian teenagers.

The abstinence-only education of my public schooling paired with the purity culture conversations I had with white evangelical Christian friends. Together these spoke to my perfectionism and internal self-loathing. They gave me a false sense of control and smugness that covered up my childhood wounds. I believed this form of complete self-denial was the only way to ensure that my adulthood could be better than my violent childhood.

Purity culture intentionally targeted youth. It sought to empower youth to live righteously for Christ through an education based in fearmongering and shame. In December 1987, research began on a Christian sexual education project inspired by 1 Thessalonians 4:3–5: "For this is the will of God, your sanctification: that you abstain from sexual immorality; that each one of you know how to control your own body in holiness and honor, not with lustful passion, like the gentiles who do not know God." Five years later, the Southern Baptist Convention (SBC) released the True Love Waits curriculum. This program would become the hallmark of purity culture. Conservative evangelical historians claim that this curriculum was a necessary response to the AIDS epidemic and the high teen-pregnancy rate, which they believed was a moral judgment from the sexual revolution of the 1960s and '70s. This curriculum and others like it relied on coercing youth to sign purity commitment cards to symbolize their spiritual and physical commitment. The goal was to get 100,000 youth to sign purity commitment cards before the next SBC annual meeting. At the 1994 convention, 102,000 commitment cards were displayed on the front lawn of the Orlando Convention Center. It took one year to ignite this movement. Over a decade later, the CDC Family Growth Report for the years when the True Love Waits movement ignited—1988 to 1995—stated that male and female teenaged sexual activity "declined significantly among those who were Protestant, those who attended religious service at least weekly, and those who lived in the suburbs."[3]

In order to combat those threats, the curriculum attacked the most sexual organ in our bodies—our brains—during one of its most vulnerable periods of development. During puberty the brain is developing its subcortical and frontal regions. The subcortical structure within the brain is where we form the deep connections between our limbic structure, basal ganglia, and pituitary gland. In other words, this is a sensitive period that develops our memories, emotions, hormone production, and pleasure. At the same time, the frontal lobe of our brains is developing our capacity for deepening memories, understanding emotions, progressing our problem-solving skills, and creating a framework for our impulse control. During puberty, the brain undergoes a process called synaptic pruning in which it releases (prunes) connections that it believes are unnecessary and strengthens more important connections. Synaptic connections are subjective, and importance is labeled according to repetition and safety from external threats. In this vulnerable period, our brains are losing small amounts of grey matter that influence the ways our brains and bodies function on a daily basis.[4] Since the brain is wired for safety, it will cling tight to synaptic connections that will equip itself to remain safe.

Purity culture turned sex and sexual deviants into villains, conditioning our brains to operate primarily out of a shame-based, fear-centered understanding of our human sexuality.[5] We received rewards like purity rings, purity balls, and the celebration of our commitment cards, but we didn't receive the interactions our brains needed to develop human connection and healthy relationships. For our pubescent brains to develop in a healthy manner, we need to let go of reward systems and instead focus on developing healthy and consistent relationships where our lessons are gained in a step-by-step manner of discovery that allows the brain to build synaptic connections that promote self-trust instead of self-shame. I know that some Christians will read this and assume that I'm saying, "Let your kids have sex as early as possible." That's a misinterpretation. Sexual development is not solely about the act of sex; it's about developing self-trust and knowing healthy relationships. If you teach a child to operate in a fear-based system of survival that conditions the brain to pine after rewards, you're developing a system of dependency that wires brains toward shame, self-loathing, and disembodiment. This, too, is sexual violence.

As teens growing up with the sex-negative teachings of purity culture, we had our thoughts and core values conditioned according to the tune of panic. We were taught to believe that deviating from the lessons would be destructive. Purity culture wired our brains to normalize patterns of self-blame and self-loathing that could also be seen in the same thought patterns as somebody who has experienced childhood sexual assault.[6] Fostering these negative attitudes toward ourselves created an atmosphere where vulnerable young girls and gender-expansive people were taught to embrace a script that perpetuated powerlessness.

Meanwhile, power was given to boys as they were taught the ways of being a predator. Within the church, the authority of men and boys went unquestioned, while the pressure of accountability was placed on the bodies of women and girls. Boys were given the power to place judgment on girls' bodies and, with it, the ability to ostracize people. Fitting into the congregation meant that girls were pressured into being appealing to the boys, who had the power to sway the perspective of the congregation. Statements like "Modest is hottest"—suggesting that a girl should be attractive without showing much skin or otherwise seeming to try to draw sexual attention—became a slogan for springtime, reminding girls to keep covered even when the weather became warmer. A girl who chose to be an individual and lived in defiance of this form of patriarchal groupthink was slut-shamed, called "open" or "loose," and (in some cases) brought up to the altar to be publicly humiliated and prayed over. I once heard a youth pastor preach about a church girl who dated an unchurched boy. In that sermon he praised the boys in their congregation who said, "I was interested in dating her, but now that I know she's with an unbeliever, I can't see her the same way. I wouldn't want to be around someone like her." The pastor went on to mourn how that girl married an unbeliever and no longer goes to church. He spun her tale of woe but never admitted how he encouraged boys to speak about her unworthiness and cast her as a pariah within the church.

I think of purity culture as a gilded prison: we were given beautiful things like rings, chains, commitment cards, and parties, but all of it was a ruse to maintain our weakness through perpetuating self-denial and villainizing our self-trust. We were pawns in the agenda of white Christian nationalism, which centers an idealized image of white, heterosexual, middle-class Christian family and demonizes, shames, and shuns any threat to that—teenage pregnancy, queer identity, poverty, and the oversexualized bodies of people of color.

This is not singular to late twentieth-century white Protestantism. Purity culture borrowed from America's long tradition of utilizing panic to perpetuate economic prosperity and maintain white supremacy. In her book *Virgin Nation: Sexual Purity and American Adolescence*, historian Sara Moslener explains that rhetoric on sexual purity has been advantageous in every instance of evangelical apocalypse: "For nineteenth-century purity advocates, it offered a way to address the fear of declining Anglo-Saxon privilege; for twentieth-century fundamentalists, the threats were nuclear destruction and communist invasion; and, for later evangelicals, the paramount concerns involved the excesses of the sexual revolution coupled with lingering

Cold War concerns."[7] Beneath the manipulative urgency of white Protestant purity-culture teachings was the manic belief that extramarital sex would lead to national decline. Purity culture was not simply theology, but national security.

Like the dynamic between Zuleikha and Joseph, purity culture gives those in power permission to sexually harass those they have power over. Purity culture shows its face through Black respectability politics, the villainizing of the LGBT+ community, revoking reproductive rights, and the passing of anti-trans laws.

I failed at purity culture at the age of nineteen. I fell in love with a guy I believed was a good Christian man. Assuming we were going to get married, I decided to have sex with him. I thought that God would let it slide that I didn't follow the order of events laid out in evangelical teachings. With the expectation of being a young bride at the forefront of my young mind, I assumed that I had healed from my years of self-loathing. Our relationship didn't last long. Unexpectedly single, I succumbed to the shame narratives I created with my childhood PTSD and Christian upbringing, then sought to silence that shame by having more sex with different partners. My distorted and traumatized mind believed that if someone could accept my body, then maybe I'd learn how to accept myself. I was no longer attending an evangelical church where I knew a leader would teach me otherwise. Instead, I started to attend a small Black Missionary Baptist church.

My experience with purity culture was vastly different in the Black church than it was in the white church. Sexual abstinence was still the main message, but I wasn't initially shunned for not being a virgin. I felt loved by our church elders, and our pastor preached in a way that didn't direct me to weakness. Purity wasn't tied to panic or powerlessness. In my Black Baptist church experience, purity culture teachings felt protective. And I, rarely given the opportunity to know protection, embraced it.

The caveat in this story is that I was also attending a sex-positive university that provided great sexual health education. While the approach to purity in my Black church context helped me feel safe enough to confess my supposed wrongdoings, I was still living my heaux tales.** I found myself stuck in an ongoing cycle. I would jump from self-loathing to sexual activity to more self-loathing to confession to a small spiritual high and fall back into the self-loathing that started the whole cycle. I was a mess. Despite my messy ways and heaux excursions, I still felt loved enough to return to my small Black Missionary Baptist church every Sunday.

Protection was at the heart of purity culture within my experience in the Black church, but it wasn't the type of protection rooted in love. It was protection from the scrutiny, judgment, and violence that came from whiteness. Being respectable protected us from the violence of whiteness and its penchant for terrorism against our Black bodies. Respectability was achieved through marriage because in order to be safe we had to be as close to whiteness as possible. We bought into purity culture because the Christian white middle class already enforced purity culture as their standard, and (in the way we theologized in that time) it was safer to deny our bodies than it was to pursue an embodied liberation. Our church elders and pastors were influenced by the words of televangelist Juanita Bynum and her "No More Sheets" testimony and subsequent sermons. Bynum led the belief that marriage wasn't simply a mark of holiness but also a cultural necessity. We Black women, with so many odds stacked against us, would not achieve the supposed blessing of entering the middle-class American dream without marriage. This was the Black church's answer to the sociopolitical landscape of the time. In the decades before Juanita Bynum came to us, Ronald Reagan ran his 1976 political campaign on the welfare queen stereotype that mischaracterized single Black mothers as villains who fraudulently collected and misused welfare payments during a time when the American economy was struggling. (He conveniently ignored the fact that most single-parent families in America at the time were white.) He was so successful in demonizing public aid that by his second term Reagan cut aid to the American Families with Dependent Children program, food stamps, and Medicaid. Working-class single-parent families fell

---

**This is a reference to Jazmine Sullivan's album *Heaux Tales*, in which Jazmine and other Black women share their stories of past relationships and discuss themes of feminism, sexuality, classism, and body shaming.

deeper below the poverty line, and those families led by Black and non-Black moms of color were disproportionately impacted.

When I inhabit my most compassionate self, I can hold love and understanding for the ways our small Black Missionary Baptist church, which defiantly resided in an affluent, majority-white beach town, embraced purity culture as a means of freedom. I can hold forgiveness and say, "I don't agree with it, but I understand why you did it." Most days I am not compassionate. I am disappointed in how we told ourselves that appealing to whiteness's pursuit of sexual disembodiment would be liberative for us. I am angry with how we deemed it holy to police our Black female bodies. We were taught to be women desperate for the redemptive quality that marriage brings, but that teaching was a fallacy rooted in the colonial structures that devalued our blessed Black bodies and turned us into Jezebel tempt-resses from the moment we were born. The enslavers' theology could only perceive Black women as commodified breeding tools that would birth a new generation of unpaid labor, and our form of purity-culture theology was nothing more than a lie rooted in this twisted psychosis that viewed us as capital and labor to be consumed for sex. In her book *Jezebel Unhinged*, womanist scholar Tamura Lomax explains that Black women don't get the benefit of making "poor choices"; instead, we carry the legacy of the enslaver's delusion that we are to be perceived as the absence of moral possibility.[8] Our pur-suit of our purity was not for the purpose of learning how to love our-selves but was rooted in protection from the enslaver's lynching tree.

What stings most is knowing the role our church had in uplifting our already small Black community. We had cookouts, held tea par-ties, and hosted NAACP meetings in the church garden. We were the safe place for Black women to scream, shout, cry, and release all the emotions we weren't allowed to express outside of the church walls. It is ironic that our praise was so embodied, and yet we couldn't embrace that embodiment in our sexuality. Moreover, it is ironic and disappointing that we embraced a sexual ethic forced upon our enslaved ancestors telling us that Black love is best achieved when Black men are dominant and Black women must combat the objecti-fication of the white gaze before we can be humanized. I don't want this for us. I want our theology to be rooted in a healthy sexuality that practices consent and care. I don't want us to continue making prisons of bodies while proclaiming these enslavers' tactics as holy living.

We must admit that sex is a part of our lives, instead of binding away our genitals in faulty chastity promises. Purity culture and abstinence-only education is restrictive, not protective. Restricting the body won't protect us from preventable consequences like sexually transmitted infections (STIs) and extramarital pregnancy. A 2021 CDC report shows that 91 percent of new HIV infections in the United States occur through heterosexual contact, and Black women have the highest infection rate.[9] If the Black church is about protecting the community and the culture, then we must have comprehensive nonjudgmental sex education that will provide protective care for Black women that is rooted in love. Nurse practitioner Michelle Breunig explains that it is a necessity for the Black church to implement an STI intervention curriculum for its youth. "Faith-based communities serve as a beacon of light in the community, play a vital role in health promotion, and provide a strong sense of support and connection in [African American] communities," she writes. "Establishing relationships with congregants in [African American] communities is a reasonable step toward executing evidence-based, ethnically, and contextually competent sexual risk-reduction and health promotion strategies."[10] I must ask those of us in the Black church if it is right for us to pursue a false righteousness that appeases the ethos of the enslavers' descendants instead of protecting us from preventable harm.

After college, I returned to my family's house in Southern California and eventually to the white evangelical church I had attended in my high school days. Barely twenty and drowning in years of practiced self-loathing, I was quick to return to repeating the purity culture scripts and one-liners I had learned in both the white and the Black church. This time, though, I had a boyfriend who left our college beach town to live in Southern California with his parents to be near me. Thus began the next stage of purity culture for us: marriage.

Christianity's obsession with sex creates an infatuation with marrying young. A 2021 survey from the Pew Research Center shows that of all religious groups in America, white evangelicals were the only religious subgroup with a majority believing that prioritizing marriage and having children would be better for society.[11] Evangelical Protestants also have the highest rates of marrying between the ages of eighteen and twenty-nine.[12] All the while, our prefrontal lobes aren't fully formed until the age of twenty-nine. I find it alarming that we're told to couple—without engaging in the necessary developmental process of dating and before we have an adequate understanding of ourselves—while we are receiving a shame script that leaves us powerless and vulnerable.

In four years of dating that man (who is now my husband), I received quite a few cringey and obnoxious one-liners:

> "Dating is sin."
> "Quit playing house."
> "Don't waste God's time."
> "You're wasting his time."
> "God wants you to get married."
> "If you've already found the person, then you shouldn't wait."
> "If you're not serious about marriage, then you're dating someone else's husband."

The message was clear: couple with intention, get the ring by spring, and have lots of Christian babies. Christian romance is transactional.

After getting married, I wish I could tell you that we had a banging sex life (pun intended), but our sex was shrouded in this false idea of piety. We prayed before having sex (which definitely ruins foreplay), and I struggled with reaching orgasm. I was so well versed in the script of self-loathing that purity culture gave me, I didn't know how to allow myself to feel pleasure. The sexual prosperity gospel had led two generations of youth to believe we'd become climaxing machines once the rings had been placed on our fingers and the vows said. That's a delusion that upholds the transactional reality of white evangelical Christianity. The church wired our brains to operate in shame and suppression, then told us that a wedding ceremony would release those bonds and lead us to the orgasmic promised land. Well, that didn't work.

Very quickly into my life as a newlywed I began to discover that these sexual malfunctions weren't only happening to me. Other young brides were pulling me aside and whispering their stories of disappointing sex, painful experiences, and misunderstandings of anatomy. We were struggling with sex—and we talked about it in whispers, behind closed doors, and with embarrassing code words. Women didn't know their bodies and couldn't imagine what pleasure or eroticism could be allowed in their lives. They were told that sex was bad during the period in their development when their sexuality was forming. Sexual fantasy, emotional regulation, embodied coping, and impulse control were necessary parts of the development of human sexuality that purity culture suppressed, shamed, and denied. Sexual desire wasn't secondary in their marriages—it was last. Instead, we listened to the teachings of small-ego alpha male pastors who were overcompensating for their half-court hairlines. They should've gone to therapy instead of being given positions of leadership. They told us that pleasuring our husbands was biblical truth and that denying our husbands was sin. We were taught to villainize consent.

After having countless hushed conversations with fellow young brides, I realized what I hated most about purity culture: we were taught how to abstain from sex, but we were never taught how to say no or what a no would feel like in our bodies. The interwoven lessons of shame and powerlessness stole our ability to know consent.

During one conversation I had to stop and ask a young woman, "Did you know that rape can happen in marriage?"

She knew what I was implying but didn't respond.

Marital rape happens when sex is forced on a nonconsenting partner. Purity culture revoked our capacity to know consent and, instead, turned marriage into an environment where one spouse remains powerless and is consistently blamed for the other's emotional immaturity and sexual malfunction. His lack is her fault. His role was that of a godly husband, head of the household, community leader, church deacon, and all-around "good guy," while she was supposed to be a sultry and obedient sex goddess who was available at his whim. This opens a vulnerable spouse to the halo effect. In her book *Prey Tell*, Tiffany Bluhm describes the halo effect as "the internal struggle to believe someone deemed as 'good' is in reality capable of doing harm [and thus he] remains in unsullied power."[13] Women weren't given the tools to name harm because the sexual prosperity gospel twisted the understanding of relationship to believe that the title "Christian man" was equivalent to moral goodness that didn't need to be questioned or held accountable. The delusion that a young virgin instantaneously becomes the "smokin' hot wife" allows marriage to be a dynamic in which marital rape is not only normalized but highly encouraged as a spiritual obligation that upholds the sanctity of the faith.

I wish I could tell you that there is a way to dismantle purity culture in one fell swoop. There isn't. The system is complicated and will continue to replicate itself every time the white middle class perceives itself to be under threat. In my teenage and college years, purity culture focused on youth abstinence, and we're now understanding the harm it has caused as more victims speak their truth. What do we do to protect ourselves, each other, and the next generation from the harm of this theological fallacy?

I've attended a few workshops on healing from purity culture that provided great tips on embodied healing and affirming one's sexual identity. I have led a few workshops on healing from purity culture that implement three- or five-step programs for embodied healing. But these workshops are incomplete without addressing the white Christian nationalist root of purity culture. Healing initiatives that center the restoration of individuals without giving them the vision or tools to dismantle the system that caused oppression is not liberative. My experience in white evangelicalism showed me that purity culture was rooted in white supremacy and the preservation of the white middle class. My experience in the Black church showed me that purity culture was rooted in perpetuating respectability as a form of protection from white terrorism. It is my belief that healing from purity culture should invite you into becoming an abolitionist because we now know how harmful it is to police bodies in favor of a racist and classist system. To authentically do so we must follow the lead of those whom purity culture demonized: Black women. If we're really going to heal from purity culture, then we must dismantle the ways that we've internalized whiteness and patriarchy, normalized policing, enslaved ourselves to capitalism, and turned the middle class into a symbol of salvation.

Far from being the virtuous and victimized Joseph in this Bible story, the church's white male leaders are in fact Potiphar's wife. They make justifications for committing sexual violence against those without power. The church's pursuit of a moralistic sense of holiness created a system that preyed on the vulnerable and made rape justifiable. We've been an active part of this culture, but we can do the work to dismantle it. Zuleikha's story doesn't have to be ours. I fear that if we don't do the work of rerouting away from white Christian nationalism, then the church will become the same as Potiphar's wife: many will know the violence done instead of the character of the God that was defamed.

Chapter Five

Rahab

Then Joshua son of Nun sent two men secretly from Shittim as spies, saying, "Go, view the land, especially Jericho." So they went and entered the house of a prostitute whose name was Rahab and spent the night there. The king of Jericho was told, "Some Israelites have come here tonight to search out the land." Then the king of Jericho sent orders to Rahab, "Bring out the men who have come to you, who entered your house, for they have come to search out the whole land." But the woman took the two men and hid them. . . .

[Rahab said,] "Now then, since I have dealt kindly with you, swear to me by the LORD that you in turn will deal kindly with my family. Give me a sign of good faith that you will spare my father and mother, my brothers and sisters, and all who belong to them and deliver our lives from death." The men said to her, "Our life for yours! If you do not tell this business of ours, then we will deal kindly and faithfully with you when the Lord gives us the land."

Then she let them down by a rope through the window, for her house was on the outer side of the city wall and she resided within the wall itself.

—Josh. 2:1–4, 12–15

grief writes a letter

my child // my strength,

tongues form to euphony of grief; allow patience
in this this this process. for it is {i am at} dusk.
there are not many sunrises left for me. I write
my blood and bones into letter. there's much to
speak of you: child of promised lands, son
of a sex worker, distanced from enslavement
and war. your life a fluttering irony blooming.
{remember remember} elders and ancestors
who dreamed seedling dreams.   we beg for
sprouting in you {remember remember} survival is a genius that morality cannot see.

grant yourself permission to trust wisdom of a businesswoman. whore.
savior. refugee. farmer. outsider. I am your mother. many people exist
within me. all are surviving unapologetically, a laughing cloudless sky.
{remember remember} how you also contain multitudes: my eucalyptus
tree amidst shrubs of desert(ed) people.

being a gravesite is a
difficult blessing.
you
are the one who will
{remember remember}
people
you never met.
whole constellations
of sadness
are needing your
visit.
Genocide
rewards us
with   griefmemory.

Conquest

In 1492 Columbus sailed the ocean blue.
He raped women, children, and animals too.

The story didn't end there, of course. He tortured Indigenous people into submission, just to feed his own ambition, and led 50,000 to commit suicide because to him their suffering was justified. He foolishly left behind his journal, so we'll know his evil ways eternal. The purpose of conquest is to amplify one's wealth through force. Conquest consumes nations, natural resources, peoples, and histories until all that is left are abused lands, diminished resources, and survivors who carry the trauma that comes with invasion. One of the greatest threats to our earth's well-being and humanity's flourishing will continue to be the justification of conquest. It parades itself as adventure and curiosity. History has imagined a great romance in taking a ship, sailing into the unknown, and claiming a new paradise for God and country. The conquest narratives we know are told with clichés like "taking a leap of faith," "burning the ships," and "God's will being done." A conquest narrative disguises itself as a faith-filled testimony to justify the atrocities it's done. Within a conquest narrative are bloodlust and sexual desire buried in a shallow grave. If I've learned anything from having the misfortune of reading Christopher Columbus's journals, it is that a conqueror is often led by misplaced religious zeal and a libido strong enough to sail a ship between continents.

Being a Californian gives me a different relationship to this truth, because this state that I live in and love dearly is named after the sexual fantasy that kept the Spanish settlers motivated during their seafaring journey. The name *California* comes from the bestselling Spanish novel *Las Sergas de Esplandían* written by Garci Rodríguez de Montalvo. In this tale, there is an island of Black women warriors led by Queen Calafia, a virgin Black Muslim warrior queen who protects the land's gold, gemstones, and other natural resources. In the novelist's words:

> Know you that to the right of the Indies there was an island called California. It was very close to the region of the Earthly Paradise, and it was populated by black women, without one

man among them, for their manner of living was almost like the Amazons. These women had strong bodies and valiant hearts burning with great energy. The island itself was full of more crags and rugged hills than could be seen anywhere else in the world. The women's armor was made entirely of gold, as was the trim on the wild beasts they rode after taming them. And there was no other metal of any kind on the entire island.[1]

When conquistador Hernan Cortés arrived at the unceded territory of the Guaycura and Pericú nations, he told his crewmates they arrived at the mythical island filled with Black women without a single man. He named the unceded land California, after de Montalvo's mythical island inhabited by the desirable Queen Calafia and her warriors. Cortés set himself and his crew on a pursuit to find her. Cortés saw more than twenty members of his crew die of starvation or hostility from the Indigenous peoples once they settled, but he clung to the myth of conquering Queen Calafia and her Black women warriors and subduing them for Christianity.

The Bible's conquest narratives likewise don't stray far from sexual fantasy. Invasion is just as much an extension of the libido as it is a figment of materialism and greed. It's not the damsel in distress that motivates colonizers; they go after the whore who needs to be tamed. What I see in the conquest narrative of California is similar to what I read in the story of Rahab.

Let me first clarify that, despite the problematic nature of conquest narratives, I do not want to villainize the orators of the Hebrew Bible, nor do I want to promote antisemitic theologies. Most of the Bible was written during the times when the Israelites were enslaved, exiled, or exploited. Their stories are not standalone narratives built on facts and evidence. Instead, they portray the ways a story can give hope to an oppressed people. The story of Rahab reflects the narrative of military might associated with entering the promised land. From Joshua and Rahab to Samson and Deborah to Saul and David—these stories were told to give hope to a people who lived in exile under the militaristic rule of Babylon. Just as the story of Adam and Eve is a cautionary tale to a nation in exile, so too were these stories of military victories told to keep the children of a nation alive during exile and occupation.

Stories are how we survive, and survival can call us to be extra petty. I understand these stories as ancient trash talking made to bolster the pride of a hurting people. My years of being overworked, undervalued, and extremely exhausted has taught me that pettiness requires creativity. I can't trash talk or clapback with literal language; the imagination must be expansive enough to one-up another person, place, or people. Imagination forms our theology. An imagination in captivity will form a theology that favors violence to make up for the harms we've endured. We must approach these texts of ancient clapbacks with care and caution: the care to recognize that these are stories built from pain to form hope, and the caution to know that we are not the main characters who were given the green light to enact violence. For far too long people of privilege and power thirsting for conquest and victory have read these narratives and assumed the message is for them.

I once heard an interpretation of the conquest narratives as "divine judgment" instead of genocide. This interpretation, of course, came from a white man who had no business speaking. This is the reality of enslavers' theology: it makes excuses for the harm seen in the Bible so the enslavers can turn around and cause the same destruction themselves. Native genocide, enslavement, the Holocaust, child trafficking, ecoterrorism—at different points in history these atrocities were labeled as "divine judgment" so that certain Christians could continue acting on their worst impulses. I don't have an issue with the ancient nation of Israel's conquest stories. I understand why the stories were created, who they were created for, and how their creation helped a people survive. My issue is with the Christo-European settlers, colonizers, and enslavers who approached these texts as directives that justified conquest and deathmongering. These stories were not for them, and yet they made the stories about them. Behind these people is the trail of death and destruction.

It is with this acknowledgment that I want to hold Rahab and see her for all that she is: a survivor, businesswoman, auntie, advocate, and hero.

Cortez's novel filled the imagination of conquistadors, encouraging them to see land and women with the same conquest-driven lens. They are the object of sexual fantasy calling listeners deep into the story. That is the role intended for Rahab, but she breaks free from the box Joshua puts her in. I have been in many Christian circles where women would raise their hands and say something like, "I am Rahab!" as if being a sex worker is the ultimate shame. They share their testimonies of being spiritually promiscuous women who eventually dedicated themselves and their families to the Lord. I love a good transformation story, but this narrative doesn't do it for me. It's sad to see Rahab, a woman who is so complex and interesting, be seen in the only dimension that serves the male libido and completely erases her identity.

I find it interesting that we don't know how she became a sex worker. Christianity has taught me that any form of sex work is wrong. But there's a difference between sex work and human trafficking. I agree that human trafficking is wrong and truly demonic, but I don't think Rahab is a trafficking victim.

There are a few parts of Rahab's story that I find deliciously interesting. There's no pimp in Rahab's household or in her story. The skeevy king of Jericho trusts her enough to send his messengers directly to her. Once the two spies of Israel get to her place of business, they "sleep" and discard their mission (Josh. 2:8). The word translated as "sleep" is important to understanding Rahab's story. As Hebrew scholar Wil Gafney explains, "The verb *sh-k-v* means to lie down for sleep and sexual intercourse. And while men (or women) may in fact sleep in a brothel; they do not generally seek out brothels as places to sleep. Those hourly rates add up and, in a brothel, beds and other flat surfaces aren't for sleeping; they're for working."[2] Three things become clear: Rahab was self-employed, she was so good at her job that she had prime real estate (the wall of a fortress), and she knew enough geographic and political secrets of Jericho to satisfy two spies of Israel. Rahab isn't a victim. She's a businesswoman who is doing what she can to survive in a place of extreme patriarchy and violence.

Becoming an abolitionist taught me that there's a difference between trafficking, survival sex, and consensual sex work. Trafficking is done under violence of force, fraud, or coercion. Survival sex can happen with or without an adult pimp. There is still a power dynamic and violence in these situations, but sex workers who are doing survival sex chose this life because other financial options were not as available to them. The reasons for being involved in the sex trade are closely related to survival: unsafe home, no available housing, lack of access to employment, poverty, misogyny, and so forth. Sex work is when someone has the capacity to choose sexual intimacy, interaction, and activity as a career choice without having threats, financial instability, deportation, or imprisonment looming over them. "It's important to not assume that every young person who trades sex for money is trafficked," writes abolitionist Miriame Kaba. "Doing so ignores the complexity of their experiences—and does a disservice to them by denying them any agency or self-determination, including to define their own experiences and demand their own solutions."[3] Rahab wasn't trafficked. I go back and forth between wondering if she was doing survival sex or sex work. Either way, it is clear to me that her business was conducted of her own volition.

Christianity taught me to pity the persons who sell their bodies. I was taught to believe they were amoral victims needing to turn away from this life and seek a disembodied salvation. Rahab teaches me there isn't one singular narrative associated with sex work. Rahab's sex work allows her to gain and share intel. Her sexpionage is an important part of dismantling the city of Jericho.

Rahab's work doesn't exploit her. We exploit Rahab by assuming she's a victim instead of celebrating how she uses her survival genius.

I rarely use the word *sin* because it misses out on the nuance necessary to affirm survival. When I decide to use it, I am intentionally doing so to attribute it to people and institutions enforcing harm through developing hierarchies of belonging. Sex work is not a sin, because this is how some persons are surviving in a society that created barriers to their flourishing. Let's recognize that morality exists in our survival. Abusing the word *sin* would proclaim that victims are morally bankrupt and remove blame from those who cause and benefit from harm. The morality is in not allowing the harm experienced by oppressive peoples and systems to live on through us. Rahab's sex work isn't a symbol of moral bankruptcy; it's evidence that she is a woman determined to provide care in whatever way that allows financial flourishing. For her, it's sex work. She's a successful businesswoman who can negotiate a deal under whatever pressure is placed on her. I love how direct her negotiating style is. She clearly explains what she wants: to have her and her family shown kindness through the protection she and her family received during Jericho's fall. She makes no mistake in explaining who her family is when she gives her commands to the spies: "that you will spare my father and mother, my brothers and sisters, and all who belong to them and deliver our lives from death" (Josh. 2:13). The spies name only her parents and brothers when they make the oath, but Rahab demands her sisters, nieces, and nephews be safe as well. She negotiates a covenant of security to ensure that all of her family members survive, not just the ones favored by militaristic patriarchy. Rahab names the women and children, knowing they would be overlooked. As a sex worker, she knows something about being overlooked, undervalued, and silenced. Survival has given Rahab the tools needed to advocate for herself and her community. Her heroism is not separate from her sex work; it exists *because* of it.

Once the spies leave Jericho, they report their intel to Joshua. It is Joshua who announces that they will remain accountable to their oath of safety made to Rahab (Josh. 6:17). They climbed down from her window with a scarlet rope. After they left, Rahab continued to hang it outside as a reminder. The scarlet rope was a symbol of accountability toward the spies, the nation, and their God. Rahab the businesswomen is not to be trifled with when it comes to how she negotiates. It doesn't matter who the oath is with; she'll remind them of what needs to be done to fulfill it. God may have told Joshua to destroy every last person in Jericho, but she keeps that scarlet rope outside of her window as a way of saying "NOT ME." Rahab, the newest member of this community of freed slaves and asylum-seeking migrants, unapologetically holds the men accountable.

Accountability is uncomfortable and disruptive. It requires everyone involved to focus with unblinking honesty on the actions that cause harm. Accountability looks at the past, leans into consequence over punishment, and imagines a new path forward. I often wrestle with

Rahab's decision to keep an entire nation and their God accountable. Did she do this because she knew genocide would follow? Did she know she couldn't stop the violence and chose this as the best course of action? What I see in the text is that Rahab is holding everyone accountable to her covenant *while* the violence is happening. When I read it I feel both empowered and disheartened: it is powerful to see a woman hold an army of men accountable, and it is disheartening to see that she can't stop the pending doom. She is resigned to what will happen and has negotiated a way forward. Rahab is a woman who is powerless to stop the destruction of her people, yet she forces everyone to look directly at her. She exists between the violence of both nations. No one expected to consider keeping Rahab and her family safe during Jericho's destruction, but she makes their safety important. Does this visible symbol of accountability make a destructive God uncomfortable, mad, or emotional? It doesn't matter. Rahab is reminding everyone of who they are accountable to—her. She is now a part of God's community, and this is her first way of showing it. God understands. God does exactly what was detailed in the terms negotiated between Rahab and the spies. When Jericho falls, Joshua orders the spies to ensure that the terms of the oath have been completed. Rahab's brazenness and unapologetic advocacy remind me that in the face of a crumbling empire God will honor the oath of those who center the safety of all peoples within their community.

I often wonder about Rahab after the fall of Jericho. Moments after the destruction she becomes a refugee. Joshua orders that she and her kin be taken to a refugee camp outside of the tribe of Israel (Josh. 6:23). Her family was distant enough from the destruction of Jericho, but they weren't far enough away that they could escape the smell of her hometown burning and the stench of her former neighbors' charring flesh. That trauma is unforgettable. As our modern understanding of PTSD recognizes, with surviving comes guilt, night terrors, and the ways the body will always be processing that moment in time. Our bodies were made for sustenance and survival. They will hold onto every moment within a traumatic event and store it in the shallow places of our muscles. Our trauma does not get stored away in vaults where it can never be accessed. Instead, it lives within the body as if it happened a few moments ago.

There's one more aspect of accountability that is often overlooked in Rahab's story. To acknowledge it we have to admit that the author of this story characterizes God as the architect of genocide. I believe this depiction of God fails. These stories were written by people who caused harm, came out victorious, and depicted their God as allowing this to happen. Like Rahab, we must hold the writers of the Bible accountable. Though the narrators explain why such violence needed to be done, a "why" isn't a necessary part of accountability. A "why" will justify harm, but it won't end it. I think it's important to recognize how genocide is the working of an imagination that glorifies dominance. This type of imagination can't see a future where everyone is free. Admitting that the Bible fails has been a hard journey for me, but doing it has brought me closer to a faith that questions who is writing God's narrative and whether or not I want to trust the narrator. "Failure and mistakes are part of a process," writes Kaba. "That feels counterintuitive because when people are in pain and have been harmed, you think you have to be perfect in order to protect that person from further harm."[4] The same standard applies to how I read Scripture, wrestle with its authors, and consider the character of God. Combatting and challenging the many authors of the Bible helped me rediscover God's character. Because I believe in a God of redemption, I also believe we can read through the violent parts of the Bible and bring its writers into accountability.

In my journey through Christianity, I've heard a lot of talk about repentance and very little acknowledgment of the need to make amends. In these pitiful teachings, repentance often takes the form of a botched-up apology in which someone justifies their wrongdoing and becomes an apologist for the harm they've caused. It infuriates me. These half-hearted confessions try to sanctify hurt instead of recognizing where wrongdoing occurred and where healing still needs to happen. Testimonies become a spectacle. The bigger the hurt, the bigger the repentance, the more active that person's spiritual life must be—as if the confession alone was a mark of spiritual sanctification. Oftentimes this came with an inflated ego: "Look at what God is doing in *my* life." I've rarely heard the admission of truth: "This is the trail of harm that will follow me if I don't make amends."

In *An Abolitionist's Handbook*, Patrisse Cullors explains, "Amends is making a plan to undo or heal the harm done."[5] It is not a quick patch to cover up the wrongs done, and it does not gaslight with statements like, "But that happened in the past and you need to get over it." Accountability does the work of sitting in recognition of the harm that was caused and not looking away. This process cannot be rushed, because it is necessary to understand what healing looks like. Healing can look like consequences, boundaries, community action plans, resources, or gifts intentionally given for restoration. When amends are made, they must be done with the intentionality of healing at the center.

Amends can be done on a personal level or on a systemic level. Amends done at the systemic level become reparations. "Reparations is not about individual harm or wrongdoing," explains Lisa Sharon Harper. "It is about state-sanctioned murder, rape, mutilation, disenfranchisement and silencing. It is about the state's sin against people groups through unjust law, policy and structure."[6] During Rahab's time, the nation of Israel was a theocracy, making God the highest level of authority. When God gave Rahab land, God performed reparation.

Rahab's having a portion of land to care for is God's way of making amends for the destruction caused to her home and the mass murder of her people. Rahab models what it means to be powerless and still require accountability from those in the position of power. God models amends by allowing Rahab to live in Israel and remain connected to her land (Josh. 6:25). This is what reparations can look like.

Reparations is the process of making amends through the double-sided work of action and monetary giving. In Rahab's time, land meant wealth, security, and longevity. God created land to be an equitable resource that works in a reciprocal relationship. The land provides for us, and we were created to care for it. Remaining on the land is God's reparation to Rahab. It was to provide wealth, security, and longevity to her, her children, and the generations that follow.

The U.S. government—helmed by white supremacy and Christofascism—has used the biblical conquest narrative to justify its genocide and terrorism against Indigenous and Black peoples inhabiting this land. If they can white-knuckle these stories to justify their own violence, then we too can use these stories to hold them accountable for issuing reparations in the same way that God did to Rahab. God did it; they can too.

If reparations can happen in Rahab's timeline, then I am foolish enough to demand that reparations be given now to me, my family, my community, and to my Indigenous kin. I am crazy enough to write these words and encourage whoever reads them to see what God has modeled for us in the margins. I am learning to be shameless in not settling for less than what is needed for healing. Healing the pain of our Black and Indigenous communities requires accountability, apology, and amends by those who are currently benefiting from the atrocities of the past. Money must be given. Land must be returned. Predatory lending practices, unnecessary punishment, community divestment, and mass incarceration must all come to an end.

We must become brazen enough to unapologetically demand, conspire together, and organize for reparations to be given. Accountability and expectation for amends can be an uncomfortable pursuit, but harm will not end unless we stand in the discomfort and demand to receive the same things Rahab got.

As much as I love the story of Rahab rescuing her family, I also know how focusing on this story gives us an incomplete view of who she is. Rahab's life is divided into two parts: the first is her life as a sex worker from fallen Jericho, and the second comprises her roles as an ethnic minority in Israel, a genocide survivor, and the mother of Boaz. While she isn't mentioned alongside Boaz in the book of Ruth, her essence exists in how her son operates. I won't lie—I'm a fan of the love story within the book of Ruth. I also know that Boaz is somebody's son. Rahab's indigenous identity and sex positivity is essential to the love story between Ruth and Boaz. It's riddled with unmistakable characteristics of Rahab as a mother: deep affection, business savvy, and bucket loads of sexual tension.

Rahab reminds me of the mothers and aunties who preserve the ways of their nations through how they raise their children. For survivors of genocide, being able to raise our children is a form of resistance. Mothering—which includes caregiving, community organizing, and youth development—is liberative action and transformative justice. It doesn't always feel like it. I spend most of my time changing diapers, dealing with tantrums, and intervening when my kids disagree with each other. Most days I am too tired to wonder if I am mothering my children to be compassionate leaders who are defying the opinions of conquerors and pursuing an abolitionist reality. But I am quickly reminded that I am mothering my kids in an imploding country. Currently, political news correspondents are saying that we're witnessing a judicial coup from the U.S. Supreme Court. There are Christofascist nationalists who are hellbent on violence, conquest, and forming an ethnocentric state. Our Asian American elders and women are being targeted for heinous violence from vigilantes. It feels like there is another mass shooting every week. LGBT+ people are being demonized and attacked. The police, emboldened with more rights and less accountability, are actively killing Black and non-Black people of color and using our children for target practice. Like Rahab, I am mothering from a place of preservation and survival.

When mothering is set to the tune of survival, children learn to make the ways of hyper-awareness and self-preservation their second nature. "Parents who have experienced trauma often have excessive feelings of fear and worry that an unnamed catastrophic event is going to happen," writes Inger Burnett-Zeigler. "So they try to exert control over their children in an attempt to keep them safe from harm. This behavior is intended to protect children, but instead, the adults model anxiety and the children internalize the fears and worries of their parents as their own. The fears of the parents become the fears of the children."[7] In the book of Ruth, we see the ways Boaz maneuvers and manipulates rules to care for Ruth. He instructs his workers to leave grain for her (Ruth 2:8–9). He tends to her basic needs for survival (2:14–16). He protects her reputation after they have sex (3:14–18). He negotiates becoming her husband despite not being in the line of succession to do so (4:2–12). Boaz, the son of a sex worker, saw Ruth and knew what hardship she could endure as a Moabite woman among the Hebrew people. He knew how to tend to Ruth's survival because his mama infused her survival skills into him. There is deep love in the relationship between Ruth and Boaz, but deeply coded within is an Indigenous mama who understood fear as a constant friend and taught her son how to prosper and survive.

I cling tightly to Rahab because I am in the vulnerable spaces of motherhood, accountability, oversexualization, surrender, and resistance. It is heart-wrenching to raise my three children during the ongoing collapse of an empire. It is exhausting to live in this multiple identity of oversexualized object within a male fantasy. I often look to her when I feel like I'm falling apart; what she models in survival is a blueprint of faithfulness.

Rahab protected her family as her society crumbled.

Rahab chose to hold an army accountable in the face of death.

Rahab received reparations.

Rahab didn't get the benefit of owning her story, but her genius shined through how she mothered her children and her community.

The period after the murder of George Floyd was when I had to make my Rahab decision. During this time when evangelical churches were either silent, gaslighting, or making false promises, I had to decide how I wanted to survive. My community of justice-centered women held a small candlelight lament vigil for us to release every grief we held onto. The white male pastor of the white evangelical church I attended at that time attended our lament vigil and mourned with us. I won't deny that his heart also ached at the video of Floyd's murder. He too desired justice and change. But I knew his ache and desire were far different from my own. The pastor said something I cannot forget: "I want to gently lead our congregation to the work of racial reconciliation. Think of it like a cruise ship; it does not turn abruptly. Turning a ship is slow and gentle."

At the time, I listened and nodded, because I didn't have the language to tell the truth. I do now: this "slow and gentle" strategy appeals to the comfort of the privileged and doesn't care for the role they take as executioners. Too many people die when any church decides to be "slow and gentle" with issues of injustice. Too many people have died already.

A few weeks later I left that church. I just couldn't get that metaphor out of my head. *The church is a cruise ship. The church is a cruise ship. The church is a cruise ship.* It reeked of privilege and opulence. It said nothing about the people who were drowning in the waters they glided on. I tried to move slowly with the ship. I tried to be gentle with the people who continued to raise their hands in worship and then out in the foyer celebrate migrant children being locked in cages and police officers killing Black people. I had to stop. I didn't want to associate with death dealers, and I was too tired to appeal to the humanity of people who acted as if I didn't have any.

I met with the pastor and abandoned the cruise ship.

We must be willing to admit that whiteness and Western Christianity are more like Rahab's Canaan than God's promised land. Violence is not our solution. Truth is, I don't know how to completely filter out these evils that poisoned God's living water. There are days when I don't even want to drink from these streams. I am still seeking pathways of resistance to imperialist white male patriarchal supremacy that remain accountable to human flourishing. "One must employ deimperialization with caution," write educators Allyson Tintiangco-Cubales and Edward R. Curammeng. "Processes of decolonization and deimperalization run the risk of exerting the same genocidal force upon Indigenous lands, ideas, and ways of life. Therefore, to deimperialize must not recast, appropriate, and perpetuate cultural genocide . . . in one's attempt to learn and honor Indigenous knowledges and cultures."[8] It is in this process that I am learning to be like Rahab—to speak truth, focus on my community, hold people accountable, and mother my children to become community organizers who center human flourishing.

It's been a few years since I left that evangelical church. I'm still healing, decolonizing, and building a pathway filled with questions and ponderings instead of the answers and justifications evangelical Christianity gave me. Most importantly, I'm trying to raise kids who won't grow up to perpetuate spiritual abuse and gaslighting. I am learning, failing, and being held accountable by my people throughout this process.

I met someone I will call Kuya Jo, a scholar and activist who studies indigenous education throughout Pasifika. He taught me of a new ship metaphor that speaks to my heart and dismantles the traumatic images of conquest ships and the crusty cruise-ship metaphor that my former pastor used. This ship is the balanghai. It's the canoe my Filipinx ancestors rode on as they traveled through Pasifika and traded along the Maritime Jade Road. Kuya Jo told me that traveling on the balanghai means we must intentionally say no to bringing things that would weigh down our ship. We bring onto our balanghai the people we are closely connected to, trust deeply, conspire with, and are unafraid to hold accountable. The interconnected dance of survival and flourishing requires us to remove what and who doesn't belong on our balanghai so that we can, as Kuya Jo taught me, "make space for the horizon ahead of us."

Chapter Six

Jael

Now Sisera had fled away on foot to the tent of Jael wife of Heber the Kenite, for there was peace between King Jabin of Hazor and the clan of Heber the Kenite. Jael came out to meet Sisera and said to him, "Turn aside, my lord, turn aside to me; have no fear." So he turned aside to her into the tent, and she covered him with a rug. Then he said to her, "Please give me a little water to drink, for I am thirsty." So she opened a skin of milk and gave him a drink and covered him. He said to her, "Stand at the entrance of the tent, and if anybody comes and asks you, 'Is anyone here?' say, 'No.'" But Jael wife of Heber took a tent peg and took a hammer in her hand and went softly to him and drove the peg into his temple, until it went down into the ground—he was lying fast asleep from weariness—and he died. Then, as Barak came in pursuit of Sisera, Jael went out to meet him and said to him, "Come, and I will show you the man whom you are seeking." So he went into her tent, and there was Sisera lying dead, with the tent peg in his temple.

—Judg. 4:17–22

Abecedarian of a Tent Peg to the Temple

Abolish this curse // my womb-captivity
Beckoning me—mother-whore—to
Collapse the wild entanglement of this
Disastrous assumption // Peace, I am not.
Every damneddisappointingdolting moment, un-
Forgotten blood trail lingering at each step
Give me the opportunity to
Heal the bloodline of sallowed negotiations.
I thought it would take more to kill a man, but
Jubilant are the ancestors eviscerating the rhythm of rape.
Keep the tent open // blood curdling under coagulated sky
Listen to victim's screaming from (after)life. All he wanted was
Milk and curds and pussy and calm and hiding place. I pray
No solace comes to the tyrant who st-
Ole our ability to dream. Little did they know I
Planted seeds in my ears—let
Quivering thoughts grow thorned
Roses // a freedom dream protected. My
Sanctuary began when his body convulsed to rigor mor-
Tis a shame to be murdered by the
Unlikeliest person // ME // reminding him of e-
Very mother who loved him to monstrosity.
Waitingwaitingwaiting we were, organizing a
Xenolithic moment. Praying for it with words and tears but
YHWH answers the footstepping prayers of
Zealous victims filled with rage, seeking relief.

Assimilation

When I was six, my favorite item of clothing was a black shirt decorated with the white lettering and the colorful shapes that were a nod to the font used in the 1990s TV show *Martin*. My shirt proclaimed the words "Knowledge is power." My six-year-old self would strut down that elementary school blacktop with her unfurled curls, crown of ever-resistant baby hairs, gleaming melanin, and this T-shirt manifesto made for everyone to see.

The pursuit of knowledge has been a cornerstone in my development. While my parents focused on our education, they did it from two very separate places. My childhood shirt's "Knowledge is power" slogan meant something very different to each of them. Mom nurtured us into becoming readers. She read with us when she had time and played an audiobook on cassette for us to listen to when she did not. She would take us to events at the local bookstore and ensure there were always books in our home. From her perspective, a love of reading was what gave us power. On the other hand, my dad embedded in us the power of eloquence in a world that favors whiteness. He needed us to prove that we were better than the stereotypes surrounding Blackness. At times it felt like he needed us to speak well so badly that his life depended on it. It wasn't until I entered my late twenties that I finally realized how his desperation in nurturing our eloquence *was* a life-or-death matter. When people tell me (or my brother) of how well we speak, I feel the need to add this refrain: I speak well because my dad abused us into eloquence, and yet this was the only way he knew how to love us. Survival is its own form of love. He loved my gift for language as best he could—not with tenderness, but with criticism and expectation.

My parents came by their different cultural perspectives on education honestly. My mother's education in the Philippines was conducted in English and normalized the discrimination against Philippine indigeneity. Her education was a direct product of US president William McKinley's Benevolent Assimilation Proclamation and the Philippine genocide that followed a year later. Her schooling led her to believe Tagalog was unnecessary and that our flourishing as Filipinx peoples was directly tied to our ability to assimilate to the West. My father grew up in the Mississippi Delta during Jim Crow segregation in the 1940s, '50s, and '60s. He understood that respectability and eloquence were the best avenue for survival from white supremacist terrorism in America. Education gave us the tools to gain respectability and assimilate into white imperialist cisgender patriarchal ideologies embedded within American society. The school curriculums, books, and Bible studies I learned from centered these ideologies. Knowledge is power, and I find myself reckoning with how the circulation of these ideologies within my education has empowered those who've oppressed me.

I think assimilation is the ongoing experience of heartbreak. I don't mean heartbreak in the romantic sense, as if time will heal it and we'll be able to meet someone new, but I think the experience of assimilation is generational heartbreak. I prefer Buddhist lama Rod Owens's definition: "I define heartbrokenness as a disembodied expression of disappointment that longs to be cared for."[1] Understanding assimilation as heartbrokenness allows me to grieve, heal, and connect with truer versions of myself that do not present as respectable to imperialism, whiteness, and cisgender patriarchy.

When I think of living an unassimilated life, I think of Jael. She is a woman of the Kenite tribe who liberates her people from being captured by the Canaanite army. Jael is liberator, abolitionist, and "most blessed above women" (Judg. 5:24). She does not assimilate into the expectations of imperialism, whiteness, and cisgender patriarchy that Bible interpretations force upon women. Instead, she is assertive and cunning, taking the freedom of her people into her own hands by murdering Sisera, the commander of the Canaanite army. Moreover, she does not assimilate into the standards of womanhood. Reading the work of queer theologians teaches me to appreciate the ways Jael moves through the world as someone who disregards the gender binary.

White imperialist cisgender patriarchal ideologies constructed a sociology of gender to operate in the binary that only offers the ultimatum of boy or girl, and over the past few hundred years these two gender categories were impressed around the globe, turning gender into a forecast and making white patriarchy the permanent weatherman ruling over our lives. "Gender is one of the biggest projections placed onto children at birth, despite families having no idea how the baby will truly turn out. In our society, a person's sex is based on their genitalia," writes George M. Johnson, a Black and queer activist and memoirist. "That decision is then used to assume a person's gender as boy or girl, rather than a spectrum of identities that the child should be determining for themselves."[2] The gender binary doesn't exist in many cultures outside of Western colonialism: some examples of genders beyond male and female are the Bakla in the Philippines, Muxe in Mexico, the Fa'afafines and Faafatamas in Samoa, the Whakawahine of the Maori in New Zealand, the Sekrata in Madagascar, the Burrnesha of Albania, the Bangala of the DR Congo, and the Metis in Nepal. I am naming this because those who subscribe to colonial Christianity and white Christian nationalism refer to gender-expansive identities as a "new" or "trending" threat, but there is nothing new about them. Jael's unassimilated, nonbinary gender identity is indicated in the biblical text of her story.

I am Jael's fangirl. She is in a small category of women in the Bible who kill their oppressors and receive blessing for doing so. As I read her story, I wonder if Jael can be considered a victim of sexual exploitation. Jael is a person living in a time of war, and sexual violence is a tool of war. The UN says that sexual violence needs to be treated as a war crime: "According to UN Action Against Sexual Violence in Conflict, the vast majority of casualties in today's wars are among civilians, mostly women and children. Women in particular can face devastating forms of sexual violence, which are sometimes deployed systematically to achieve military or political objectives."[3] For Jael, living in a time of war meant that her body and the bodies of others were in constant threat of being sexually exploited by those seeking military gain. While I am committed to liberation through nonviolent action, I believe that Jael's actions serve as a reminder that freeing myself and my people means we don't have to subscribe to assimilation to ensure our safety. We can dismantle what intends to destroy us by metaphorically taking a tent peg to its temple.

Jael is first alluded to in the book of Judges by the prophetess Deborah after Barak, Israel's military leader, says that he will follow the Lord's commands so long as Deborah rides alongside him (Judg.

4:8). Deborah recognizes that Barak has become dependent on her presence rather than the Lord's word and proclaims that he will not be the one to defeat Sisera. Instead, "the LORD will sell Sisera into the hand of a woman" (4:9). When Jael is introduced in verse 17, her gender is coded as a woman because she is the wife of Heber the Kenite. Immediately afterward, however, she begins to spill into masculine-coded terms as her gender expands beyond the category of "woman." When the warmongering general needs refuge from a pending military loss, the tent he goes to is referred to as Jael's—not her husband's—and her name is presented in the masculine form, *yā'ēl*, instead of a common feminine spelling, *tā'ēl*.[4] When I first learned of this, I assumed her name was a misspelling that should be overlooked. There is no *tā'ēl* elsewhere in this Bible story; why should this spelling of her name be important? This spelling of her name characterizes her as someone who will not conform to cultural assumptions of femininity. The spelling of her name is a nod to her unassimilated life. "The importance of names for conveying information about an individual is especially true in the Hebrew Bible where names often express meaning," writes Jewish scholar Aysha M. Musa. "Biblical characters' names sometimes change in order to recognize a shift or transformation in the individual, and accordingly reflect something regarding their character."[5]

Alongside Jael's tent-property-ownership and male-coded name, Jael blurs the gender binary through her actions. Sisera seeks her for peace and comfort as he flees the battle he's losing. "Turn aside, my lord, turn aside to me; have no fear," Jael says, enticing Sisera in his moment of vulnerability and inviting him into her tent (4:18). Admittedly, I first thought she was saying this because she was going to give him a massage or scratch his back. Nope, that's not it. Jael is using the language to arouse Sisera. "Her use of the address 'my lord' may also be a bit of verbal foreplay," writes Hebrew Bible and history of Judaism professor Tikva Frymer-Kensky. "This address is often used in the Bible by women towards men with whom they have or will have a sexual relationship."[6] Jael then "covers him with a blanket," assertively taking control of the situation. This coded language is definitely an innuendo for sex. Because the sex is consensual, I will not categorize this sexual encounter as rape. It's important to note that although Sisera is the cisgender military leader, he takes on the submissive role while Jael—controlling the whole situation—becomes the masculine-coded dominant partner in their sexual encounter while still retaining the female-coded role of caretaker. She simultaneously occupies two gender roles, expanding herself beyond the binary.

Once the sex is done, Jael transitions into a new female archetype. She becomes a doting mother when Sisera shifts his needs from sex to food. He stops being the violent militaristic general and enters her tent like a vulnerable child asking for a snack and a nap, both of which Jael gives. This interaction interests me. Sisera asks Jael for water: "Please give me a little water to drink, for I am thirsty" (4:19). Instead of water, she opens a skin of milk, lets him drink, and then covers him. Scripture uses milk as a symbol of abundance and fertility (like the promised land being known as "the land of milk and honey"). Drinking milk is a symbolic act of being mothered. A war commander allowing himself to be mothered by his victim also indicates that he is like a baby drinking milk from its mother's chest. He is not in control.

At this point, Jael embodies many tropes associated with femininity, blending maternal overtones with sexual subtexts. It's strategic. Sisera, now sexed and sleepy, orders Jael to protect him as he rests. "Stand at the entrance to the tent," Sisera commands her, "and if anybody comes and asks you, 'Is anyone here?' say, 'No'" (4:20). It is assumed that Sisera is ordering Jael to take on the matronly role, but these events are happening amid war. A cisgender woman would not be expected to be at the battle because, if the army were to fail, she would instantly be a spoil of war. Sisera is requesting that Jael embody both roles in the gender binary: the feminine-coded overseer and the masculine-coded loyal soldier at wartime. Jael's breaking free from assimilation into the gender binary is essential to her murdering Sisera: "But Jael wife of Heber took a tent peg and took a hammer in her hand and went softly to him and drove the peg into his temple, until it went down into the ground—he was lying fast asleep from weariness—and he died" (4:21).

It's not enough to say that Jael's killing of Sisera is what makes her gender-expansive. Self-defense and murder are not gender-coded actions. It is *how* she kills him that defies the gender binary. The words used to describe Sisera's murder—*softly, drove, pierced, sank*—have been used in other places of the Bible to describe sexual violence.[7] Jael performs calculated sexual homicide, but not of the male form (in conjunction with rape) or the female form (done in self-defense from intimate-partner abuse or for money). Instead, she receives the masculine glory of murdering him in war. God adorning Jael with this male-specific glory is an intentional action of the Lord to expose the entrapment that is the constrictive gender binary *and* to show that gender assimilation is not a necessity in the pursuit of liberation.

Understanding the story through this queer-studies and sex-positive lens shifted the way I understood the way Deborah honors Jael: "Most blessed of women be Jael / the wife of Heber the Kenite, / of tent-dwelling women most blessed" (5:24 ESV). I once believed that Jael, the only woman to be named as blessed within the Hebrew Bible, received this praise because of her feminine power. Now that I am on my journey of freeing myself from ultimatum-based thinking, I wonder if Jael is named most blessed because she didn't assimilate to the expectations held within heteronormativity and the gender binary.

Gregory H. Stanton is the president of Genocide Watch, an organization that exists to predict, prevent, stop, and punish genocide and other forms of mass murder. He has identified ten stages of genocide: classification, symbolization, discrimination, dehumanization, organization, polarization, preparation, persecution, extermination, and denial. Stanton explains that this isn't a linear process. Rather, each stage of genocide is a process of convincing people to embrace the violent rhetoric of genocide that allows war crimes to be committed through the eradication of people from a particular nation, ethnic group, or identity.[8] There are moments in history when a genocide is complete and an entire people group is eradicated. Other times, society lingers on certain steps toward genocide, and while a mass killing doesn't happen, we are able to see a people group living for years under the threat of violent extermination.

Sisera, the commander of the Canaanite army, is one or two generations removed from genocide. The Hebrew Bible isn't clear on his lineage, but what we know of the timing between Jericho's fall to Sisera's murder is that he or at least his parents or grandparents were alive at the beginning of the conquest of Canaanites. The violence he uses to oppress Israel is colored with vengeance for his people who were slain. Scripture doesn't hold back on describing Sisera's terrorism: "He had nine hundred chariots of iron and had oppressed the Israelites cruelly twenty years" (Judg. 4:3). As a Kenite, Jael lived in proximity to the Israelites. There was solidarity between the Israelites and Kenites. Jael spent years of her life watching Israelites endure Sisera's terrorism. Living among the Israelites would have exposed her to the stories of Jericho's fall and the Canaanite genocide. I wonder if she lived in the complicated nuance of "both/and." Jael knew that *both* the Israelites and the Canaanites were violent tribes caught up in war with one another, *and* she knew that this cycle of war and genocide would continue between them.

I want to focus on Jael's solidarity with the nation of Israel. She saw wrongdoing on both ends and made the decision to end Sisera's reign of terror as a step toward a complicated form of progress. Jael's actions were calculated movements of rage against war and oppression. Liberation, in all its forms, requires rage. I like the word *rage* because it elicits a reaction from people. I like to watch how they twitch or jerk when I speak of rage. I like it because it gives me a small glimpse into what they've been taught to allow themselves to feel. If we cannot feel rage, then we cannot know liberation. If we are afraid of it, then we cannot know what life will be like beyond it. As Audre Lorde wrote, "To search for power within myself means I must be willing to move through being afraid of whatever lies beyond."[9] The moment that I was able to acknowledge my rage was the moment when I recognized all the ways I took my anger inward and deepened my own helplessness. In feeling my rage, I was able to say, "I am not the problem. This society is." I found the power within myself.

Cole Arthur Riley describes rage—or holy anger—as passionate and calculated.[10] I want to expand on this and name three elements of rage: care, community building, and reflection. Rage is what organizes the protests, it is what keeps our bodies marching, it creates policies that protect vulnerable people, it is what gives food to people starved by a government that hates the poor. Rage cares for the community that is disenfranchised by an oppressive and discriminatory governing body. Rage allows us to take part in restructuring our communities as we name and dismantle the evils of our society. Rage is a truth teller and hope seeker. The last and rarely acknowledged element to rage is reflection. The pursuit of justice cannot be sustained with the escalation that comes with the initial moments of rage. When I think of Jael—unassimilated and enraged—I see someone who moved beyond the helplessness of anger and found the power of her rage. Reflecting on rage gives us the power of feeling our feelings and disowning the shame or harm that doesn't belong to us. It allows us to expand our vision and see how we dismantle the old world and how we build a new one. Jael murdered Sisera to end his vengeance against Israel and to halt a cycle of war between the two nations. While her actions didn't end all warring between the Israelites and Canaanites, they did stop Sisera's twenty-year reign of terror.

There is deep love in rage, and through that love we can march toward revolution. Rage needs us to connect with one another in order to break our bonds to power and dominance. This is the difference between anger and rage: anger is the experience of facing a threat to human flourishing and not knowing how to heal it. It gives us energy and momentum to protect ourselves or others, but without tools or strategy that energy is unfairly disbursed. We feel angry because we feel helpless and don't yet have the tools or community that will help us choose a path void of vengeance. I have been angry for many years, but it wasn't until recently that I allowed rage to ignite within me a desire to construct a new world. To tap into my rage I must acknowledge all the ways I assimilated into white imperialist cisgender patriarchal ideologies, lest I become just like Sisera and make movements based on vengeance and repeating the cycle of violence.

Do not be afraid of your rage. Let rage run its course, because at the end of rage you will find flourishing. Lean into reflecting on the ways you've assimilated to power, then become so critical of those ways that the only option is to turn away from them. Understand that rage and love are intertwined, as they help us build new worlds through restorative communities. The rage that I see in Jael is the rage I want us all to tap into (but please don't murder people!). Rage is meant to protect, heal, love, and build a new world.

There are still days when I am hopeless. Those are the days when my rage dwindles into anger and I project the violence of the world into my soul. On those days I want to inflict violence on myself or pursue vengeance. It is hard to move from anger to rage, because it requires me to give back all the vitriol that society has impressed upon me and those I love. Assimilation is heavy on my bones, because it was the first survival mechanism I learned in a world that has enacted genocide on my ancestors and protects institutions that murder people who look, think, and move through the world like me. There is no flourishing under assimilation; it is a stronghold that must be broken.

I have a friend who designs shirts with the words "Biblical Womanhood" on them. Below the words is a picture of a nail through a skull. Every time I see it, I chuckle lightly, knowing this shirt is a statement of defiance against the gender roles enforced upon her by her conservative Christian upbringing. I think it's empowering, and I'm uncomfortable because I reject Jael as a new picture of femininity. She is more than a liberated woman. I see her as someone unassimilated to the gender binary who enacts her rage and cunning to crush an oppressive militaristic entity and halt warfare between two nations.

I need to hold Jael in this light as I watch anti-trans laws and regulations pass and witness false narratives made against our queer, trans, and nonbinary siblings. I feel hopeless when I see progenocide statements like, "Transgenderism must be eradicated," and legislation being passed to remove trans children from their homes and to ban gender-affirming health care along with books and histories showcasing gender diversity. When I think of Jael, I let my hopelessness dissipate as my rage takes over. Like her I will end an ongoing cycle of violence by silencing the terrorizer and forging a new path forward.

Chapter Seven

Bathsheba

It happened, late one afternoon when David rose from his couch and was walking about on the roof of the king's house, that he saw from the roof a woman bathing; the woman was very beautiful. David sent someone to inquire about the woman. It was reported, "This is Bathsheba daughter of Eliam, the wife of Uriah the Hittite." So David sent messengers to get her, and she came to him, and he lay with her. (Now she was purifying herself after her period.) Then she returned to her house. The woman conceived, and she sent and told David, "I am pregnant." . . .

When the wife of Uriah heard that her husband was dead, she made lamentation for him. When the mourning was over, David sent and brought her to his house, and she became his wife and bore him a son.

—2 Sam. 11:2–5, 26–27

apologia

after Ocean Vuong

she asked for it   she shouldn't have been doing that
it's her fault   the body is a temptation   deny yourselves
men are naturally visual creatures   are you sure?
deny yourselves   be holy   i thought you liked it
there wasn't any force   they dress like they want it
it's just sex   it's not force if she took off her clothes
this is carnality   forgive and forget   boys will be boys
if you can't stop it, you might as well enjoy it
i blame the party culture   it happened so long ago
that's a big punishment for 20 minutes of action
modest is hottest   just let it go   i'm not a bad person
teach a kid to watch the road before crossing it LBFM
a girl for the price of a burger   this is pragmatics
men need to be healthy and fit   R&R   you're so wet
if they don't want it make 'em feel guilty about it
i'm all you have   you'll never do better than this
for God and country   this is destiny   God chose you

Conspiracy of Silence

It was late March 2021. We were lamenting, holding each other's stories and seeing ourselves as we gathered in a secret online space only for Asian American and Pacific Islander women. It was just days after the Atlanta spa shootings, where a white terrorist, clinging tightly to the white Christian nationalist narrative of purity culture, brutally murdered eight people in three separate spas. Six of the eight victims were Asian American women. They were targeted because they represented sexual temptation for a misled desperate man who was taught a militaristic theology and wanted to be saved from his supposed sexual addictions. Instead of cleansing himself with fire, he decided to be God. He exposed the wounds we were taught to hide. Our suppressed grief deepened as the world began asking questions to answers our bodies already knew:

Why did he do it? Because he thought we were sex objects.

Was this racially motivated? Of course.

What made him think this was right? Imperialism.

Is this purity culture teaching? Yes.

Is this evangelicalism? Surely.

Is America this violent? Always.

There, in that sacred space, we didn't have to listen to questions from people who needed to settle their shock with answers. We were all women of Asia and Pasifika who were allowed to cuss, curse, cry, and rebuke lies. Our relationships to this religion were as unique, complex, and diverse as we were. What was true, what always remains true, is that we needed to heal among people unafraid to speak the truth.

"We are Bathsheba," said preacher, coach, and public theologian Erna Kim Hackett. She organized our sacred and secret healing space. From her rose these words our souls knew but couldn't grasp. We, the women of Asia and Pasifika living in the land that conquered our lands, are Bathsheba. Her story knows us and tells our experience.

What I hate most about Bathsheba's story is how we have named it "David and Bathsheba" instead of confronting what it truly is: the

rape of Bathsheba. Her story is a devastating rebuke of what happens when our spirituality is intermingled with militaristic might and
abuse of power. Rape is about power, and the story of Bathsheba's
rape exposes the complexities of how the abuse of power, privilege,
and personhood bare deep consequences. The sooner we can hear
and accept these truths, the sooner we can look at ourselves and our
spiritual spaces with the introspection that is necessary to heal ourselves and our communities.

Before David knows who Bathsheba is, he decides to target her.
After having just woken from a late afternoon nap, he walks to the
roof of his palace and sees Bathsheba bathing. David is not coerced,
nor is Bathsheba intentionally tempting him. She's cleaning herself
after her period, a ritual that invites women back into society after
their period is over. It is David's desire that motivates him to rebuke
decorum and pursue her. He uses his power to know her name and
her family, and to summon her to his palace. When they are together
and alone, he commands that she lay with him.

In this moment, Bathsheba is burdened by the reality that this is
the man who wields the power to isolate, exile, and ruin her entire
family, who has served Israel's military faithfully for generations. She
does as he requests, but not because she chooses to. Choice is erased
when the person in power propositions sex. Bathsheba is powerless.
That is a key part of the story. This is not her decision; this is David's
coercion. A yes given under pressure or threat of violence does not
equal consent. Consent must be freely given, reversible, informed,
enthusiastic, and specific.[1] Bathsheba wasn't in a position where she
could give consent. She was raped.

Time passes and Bathsheba sends word to King David, confronting him with news of her pregnancy. Her husband has been away
at war during and after Bathsheba's rape. She hasn't had sexual
relationships with anyone else. David is the father, and now Bathsheba is stuck in a twisted situation where she needs the help of her
rapist to protect her. I often think about the amount of courage it
took for Bathsheba to confront her rapist. She does not threaten to
expose him, because she knows it could lead to more violence for
her and her family. Instead, she plainly tells him the truth: "I am
pregnant." She does not blackmail David. There is no proposition

made to threaten him or their nation. She is powerless in every way, and the pregnancy is not a tactic to gain power. Her pregnancy is the revelation of David's sin. She, like so many rape victims, carries his violence within her body. Below the surface of her skin, deep within her psyche, she battles with the blame that plagues a victim. But this is not her shame to hold; it is David's. The unfortunate truth is how society would sooner blame and deny her than it would hold David accountable.

David skirts accountability. David summons Bathsheba's husband, Uriah, to return to his household so that Uriah may sleep with his wife. But Uriah doesn't; instead, he stays with other soldiers to protect their homeland and the ark of the covenant. Uriah is committed to doing what is important for their nation and their faith. When David asks why he won't return to his wife, Uriah confesses that he would be unsettled to take pleasure at home when threats loom over his country and the military he serves in. In desperation, David decides to throw a feast for Uriah so that he will get drunk and sleep with his wife. Once again, Uriah foils his plans.

Three times David plots and is denied. He is desperate because his plans to cover his sins are constantly ruined. He's also desperate because Uriah models what David, who stays in Jerusalem when he is supposed to be with his troops in battle (2 Sam. 11:1), does not. Uriah is righteous. Uriah is loyal. Uriah is dedicated. Uriah has boundaries. Here we see David's insecurities on full display: he was once proclaimed as righteous and chosen by God; now he is unraveling at the knowledge that he is no longer this man. David has spent years of his life being victorious as he battled lions, other nations, and the former king he admired. But he could not claim victory in his battle with himself. Instead, Uriah presents a new internal battle for David: the battle of returning to his former self in order to keep his glory intact. Desperate and defeated, David hatches a plan to have Uriah killed in battle. In David's eyes, covering up the truth is a better option than repentance.

After making her a widow, David takes his victim into his household. The palace becomes Bathsheba's gilded prison where she has no one to protect her or advocate for her. Bathsheba becomes David's wife, but it is a thinly veiled title to distract us from the fact that she is a rape victim who is now imprisoned by the monster who violated her.

I have listened to many sermons in which a male pastor or a patriarchal woman pastor has blamed Bathsheba. Their loyalty is to patriarchy and power. Believing victory is conquest, they hold tightly to David as the model of righteousness because their faith is too insecure to admit that he has done wrong. When given the choice between admitting fault and hiding harm done, they will go the way of David.

I have also met people who admit that David has done wrong but quickly flip to Psalm 51 and talk about David's remorse. These people stand firmly in the verses that declare how David was a "man after [God's] own heart" (1 Sam. 13:14), then they'll use Psalm 51 as evidence of that. But a man after God's own heart can fail, and that same man needs to be exposed and held accountable. Psalm 51 is a poem about failing just as much as it is a poem about redemption. It was written because David got caught. It would not exist had it not been for God's intervention through Nathan, showing David what evil he had perpetrated and warning him that the child would die (2 Sam. 12). David cared more for his desires than his sins, and more about his power and reputation than he did about Bathsheba. David pens Psalm 51 desperately seeking forgiveness and redemption from God, but it's important to recognize that David is shortsighted in his pursuits. He wants redemption from the moment so that his power can remain afterward. But God sees past this. Psalm 51 is performative. When we Christians base our theology on performative actions, our faith is nothing more than apologia for harm.

The child, whose age is not mentioned (Was it a newborn? A toddler?), falls terribly ill for seven days, during which David begs for God to change the child's fate. But what of Bathsheba? Has she grown to love their child? Has she stayed at his bedside as he has deteriorated from illness? How does it feel to be alone with servants as the child she bore lies dying and his father is elsewhere? Who is God to Bathsheba in these moments? We don't know because her story is erased. Instead, we find David performing sacrilege all while knowing the end to God's plan. But Bathsheba doesn't, and her heartache is louder than David's prayers.

Their child dies on the seventh day. Pious David pops up from his pleading to get washed, anointed, eat, and worship the Lord. There is no grief for his rape-child. Instead, David shows relief and victory. He is victorious because he feels that he no longer has the Lord's punishment looming over him. Then the most heartless and spiritually abusive words escape David's mouth as he speaks with his servants:

> Then his servants said to him, "What is this thing that you have done? You fasted and wept for the child while it was alive, but when the child died, you rose and ate food." [David] said, "While the child was still alive, I fasted and wept, for I said, 'Who knows? The LORD may be gracious to me, and the child may live.' But now he is dead; why should I fast? Can I bring him back again? I shall go to him, but he will not return to me." (2 Sam. 12:21–23)

The servants' disgust is palpable as they listen to their king justify why he won't grieve the loss of his child. They watched as he shifted instantly from despair to elation. But they, too, are unable to challenge him lest they receive their king's wrath. Instead, they watch David go to the mourning Bathsheba to console her and have sex with her. Bathsheba may be David's wife now, but she is still his prisoner, and every sexual act between them is still mired in coercion. Once again, she is raped.

There is a term that is rarely known but makes so much sense when I introduce it to other victims of sexual violence: *conspiracy of silence*. It is both poetic and devastating. A conspiracy of silence is when a group of people creates an unspoken agreement to never mention, discuss, or even acknowledge a subject. The number of people in a group may vary; it can be a small gathering of people, a family, a community, a school, a church, or an entire nation. A conspiracy of silence protects the perpetrator. The one who has caused harm gains more power as others stay silent. This adds more pain to the victim. The silent treatment, shunning, social isolation, and all the ways silence is upheld will activate the area of the brain that feels physical pain. Silence is physically painful. Those who remain silent about harm are allowing the victim's body to relive the event while also enduring the pain of physical abuse.

Silence does not cover harm; it invites more harm to happen. As the harm continues, it grows in its ferocity and viciousness. Violence cannot be stopped if accountability is snuffed by a collective agreement to be silent. David's palace was a place of silence. David was the representative of God's power, Israel's unity, and the nation's military might. Speaking up against David was to question God's authority and slander Israel's army. The prophet Nathan was the only one to confront David, but there's no evidence that he was able to connect with Bathsheba. So while Nathan did the righteous act of confronting David and holding him accountable, he did not help Bathsheba directly. He was still silent toward her as she was imprisoned in a palace shrouded in the conspiracy of silence.

My Filipinx family doesn't talk much about the past. Our elders waited until we were adults to open up about their life back home. My cousins and I have lived out our adulthoods collecting the bread crumbs of stories they leave for us. We sit around the drinking table and an uncle will talk about what it was like to raise pigs, then another will chime in about climbing the coconut trees, and then suddenly my mom is saying something about drinking the fruit from the fresh buko. Bit by bit, we second-generation children learn of our heritage and where our family comes from. It is done in the holiest place of memory—the drinking table—where we eat steak and seafood while listening to our elders weave stories with their guards down.

I once asked my mom to tell me about the Philippines when my kids and I were lounging around at her house. She shot me a look and shook her head. She wanted to enjoy the moment watching *My Little Pony* with the kids. When I asked her again, without children or the TV around us, she shook her head and sighed. She didn't want to talk about it. Those memories were too painful for her to speak about alone; it's better to remember communally with the comforts of food and family around than it is to drown in memories of the place that you loved and left. I don't ask my elders about the Philippines until two or more are gathered together. It is sanctified time when the prayer of knowing who I am is answered.

There was a story of Home that accidentally spilled from their mouths. They told the story of when they hid in caves to escape the imperial Japanese military. I later learned that this is a common thread in the histories of Filipinx families who survived World War II. Countless people hid in the mountains and caves so as not to be tortured, murdered, or trafficked by the Japanese imperialists. The anti-imperialist guerillas used their knowledge of the land to resist the Japanese. Women and girls were hidden away to protect them from becoming trafficked.

Not everyone could be protected from the imperialists. In the Philippines, it is estimated that about a thousand women and girls, some as young as eight years old, were trafficked into becoming sex slaves. It is estimated that the Japanese imperial army forcefully trafficked over 400,000 women throughout Asia. Most abduction and trafficking victims were from Korea and China; trafficking victims were also abducted from the Philippines, Taiwan, Vietnam, Thailand, Papua New Guinea, Hong Kong, Macau, modern-day Indonesia and Myanmar, Australia, and New Zealand. These victims became known as "comfort women" because the military justified the violence done to them as a necessity to ensure the strength of the soldiers. Raping women and girls as young as eight years old was the army's best tactic for ensuring military success.

Stereotypes of hypersexualized Asian women were born from the minds of warmongers who, like David, sought to satisfy their need for rest by justifying their violence. They, like David, were the figureheads of the nation's might and believed they deserved what they desired for their service. I didn't realize that the atrocity of having comfort women was an initiative that the Japanese learned from other imperialists. The source of the violence of lust and hypersexualization is in the fight for Filipinx independence in the late 1800s. Writer, activist, and facilitator Panthea Lee explains this history in her article "Sex, Death, and Empire: The Roots of Violence against Asian Women":

> When the Filipinos took up arms in a bid for independence [in 1899], the US deployed 125,000 troops to persuade them otherwise. The war lasted more than three years and devastated the country. Filipinas who had never considered sex work were forced into it as a matter of survival. And American men who had not previously known any Asian women now found

themselves in a country where most women they met worked in the sex industry.

In the Philippines, [an American] soldier could have "a girl for the price of a burger," the legal scholar Sunny Woan writes. Filipinas were viewed as so subservient that American GIs sexually denigrated them in ways they would never consider for their wives or women back home. "Filipina sex workers frequently report being treated like a toy or a pig by the American [soldiers] and being required to do 'three holes'—oral, vaginal, and anal sex."

The US military registered sex workers, regularly tested them for venereal diseases, and tagged them, like pets, reinforcing their status as less than human. The military justified this system as a matter of imperial necessity. "The idea was that the soldiers are aggressively sexual and need a sexual outlet in the military theater. And if we don't set up a system and inspect women, then they're going to get sick and then we can't fight," says Paul Kramer, a historian of US empire. "It presumes all of these things about men's sexuality and then essentially says: This is a pragmatic matter of manpower. We need men to be healthy and fit."

By the end of the American colonization of the Philippines a half century later, this ideology had spread across Asia, laying the foundation for the region's notorious sex entertainment and trafficking industries. At the end of World War II, to prevent Allied troops from raping civilians, Japan established a network of brothels and recruited 55,000 women to service up to 60 GIs a day each. Many women committed suicide, particularly in the network's opening days; after the brothels closed, the Japanese saw as many as 330 rapes a day.

Though Japan had a history of exploitative prostitution, the conscription of women as a military necessity was based on studying Western tactics of empire building.[2]

I think about the phrase "women as a military necessity" often. I roll the phrase around in my head and hold it as I consider the rape of Bathsheba.

I was once eating empanadas with a Filipina American friend—I'll call her Lina—as she told me about the time she had a panic attack in church. The white male pastor of the evangelical church in the American Bible Belt was preaching on the rape of Bathsheba. Her body grew tense as she sat in the pew and listened. The white male pastor then said, "She shouldn't have been bathing on the roof-top!" Lina got up and left the sanctuary that had become a place of violence. As she sat in the foyer, surrounded by concerned people, the only thing she could say was, "It wasn't her fault! It wasn't her fault!"

There was a season of my life when pastor's wives would tell me about the abuse they received from their husbands. Sometimes it was neglect, other times it was manipulation or physical violence. Being a pastor's wife isn't easy, they'd say. We'd sit in the pews and listen to their abuser-husbands preach the gospel. They'd talk about the spiritual warfare of everyday life and sing songs to amplify these messages: Stay on the battlefield! We are soldiers for the Lord! God will come back with the head of your enemy! We are more than conquerors! They'd preach the glory, use the gory, and convince their congregations that it was all good in the sight of the Lord. But the ones who bore the marks of the true battlefield sat in the pews, nodding at their husbands, convincing themselves that being spoils of war made them living tabernacles.

I sat in a circle of women who had experienced intimate-partner violence. Some of the women were still in these relationships but seeking a way to get out. On this night they were taking self-defense classes from a male volunteer and martial arts expert. He grew up in a domestic abuse household and became a university professor teaching courses on conflict resolution and family communication. He was there to provide the help he couldn't provide to his own mother. He led the women through self-defense scenarios they already knew: what happens if your partner grabs your wrist, what to do when there's a child in the room, and what to do when your partner pins you down while restraining your arms. I watched as he taught them how to assess risk and deescalate. The women unapologetically asked necessary questions based on scenarios they had experienced. What happens if there's a weapon? What do I do if I can't get out? What do I do when my partner threatens to commit suicide if I leave? The teacher answered each question and provided strategies for each scenario. At the end of the workshop, the women thanked him, hugged each other, ate snacks, and grew deeper in community. I sat with the program director and watched this group of women whose lives were connected with death and violence. She turned to me and said, "You know, every woman in this room has lived out those situations, and they ended in rape because the other option was to be murdered."

I once thought the atrocities of war were done elsewhere. The violence was overseas but not in our neighborhoods. I was foolish and misinformed. Wherever there is a lust for power and dominance there is war: in our country, in our neighborhoods, in our churches, and in our homes. Not too far behind the places where war exists will be the bodies of tortured women.

The objectification of women is a military necessity.

Whether the battle is in the home, being glorified from the church pulpit, or happening overseas, it is the women who are forced to carry its burden and live in the cruel silence of justification.

The house of David, though secure and blessed, was also a place where war existed. David had at least twenty sons by his various wives and concubines, leading to infighting and competition—for which women, unsurprisingly, paid the price. In 2 Samuel 13:1–22, David's daughter Tamar is raped by her half-brother, David's firstborn son, Amnon. Seeking refuge, she tells her brother Absalom what happened and seeks to inform their father of the violence. Bathsheba's rapist does nothing to punish Tamar's rapist. Two years later, Absalom takes his revenge and has Amnon murdered before trying to usurp his father's throne and being killed himself.

Poor Tamar expected comfort and retribution from her father, but she learned that a warmonger's affections can only extend as far as his ability to determine value. Tamar, now a sullied woman who spoke out against her half-brother-rapist, was no longer marriageable or valuable to King David.

When Tamar rejected the conspiracy of silence in David's household, she lost her value. I often wonder if Bathsheba consoled Tamar when Absalom failed. They both shared the secret language of atrocity and survival. While neither Bathsheba's nor Tamar's mother are mentioned in the story, I imagine it was Bathsheba who wiped the ash off Tamar's face, led her to the baths, and sat in knowing silence as she gently washed Tamar's body. Perhaps it was Bathsheba who embraced her when the other women shunned her, who understood Tamar's every gesture and said, "I believe you."

Bathsheba, a prisoner in the household of her rapist, had the ability to hold his daughter as the generational act of violence was forced upon her body. Perhaps she became a healing presence in her daughter-niece's darkest time.

The next time Scripture mentions Bathsheba, in 1 Kings 1, is twenty years after her second child's birth. There is a great struggle over who will succeed David on the throne now that he is senile. David's son Adonijah is next in the order of succession and is pursuing the crown. The prophet Nathan informs Bathsheba of Adonijah's aspiration and explains the direness of this situation to her: if Adonijah claims the throne, then she and her son Solomon will be killed so as not to confuse the order of succession. Nathan seeks Bathsheba's help in stopping him and advises her how to interact with the king so that they can receive the best results (1 Kgs. 11:14).

Bathsheba goes to King David's room and follows the advice of Nathan. By this time David is old and "unable to be warm," so his healers and advisors prescribe him a beautiful woman to lie in his bed and provide him with the warmth he needs to remain alive and comfortable. Scripture is very clear that David does not have sex with her, but he's still using his political power to objectify the body of a woman for his own comfort. All the while, his healers and advisors celebrate how her beauty and youth are a medicine to his withered body (1 Kgs. 1:3–4). So gross.

We find Bathsheba confronting her rapist while he is in bed using the body of another woman to maintain his comfort. Again, the conspiracy of silence plagues her as she sees another victim of the house of David. Bowing before this man, Bathsheba explains to David the severity of Adonijah's grab for the throne, reminding him of the promise he made to her and to God:

> "My lord, you swore to your servant by the LORD your God, saying, 'Your son Solomon shall succeed me as king, and he

shall sit on my throne.' But now suddenly Adonijah has become king, though you, my lord the king, do not know it. He has sacrificed oxen, fatted cattle, and sheep in abundance and has invited all the children of the king, the priest Abiathar, and Joab the commander of the army, but your servant Solomon he has not invited. But you, my lord the king, the eyes of all Israel are on you to tell them who shall sit on the throne of my lord the king after him. Otherwise it will come to pass, when my lord the king sleeps with his ancestors, that my son Solomon and I will be counted offenders." (1 Kgs. 1:17–21)

I find this interesting, because Scripture does not provide us with the scene where David made the promise that Solomon will sit at the throne. Some interpretations say that Bathsheba is manipulating David while he is vulnerable and unable to use his full mental faculties. I disagree. Holding those views is another form of victim blaming. In order to survive, Bathsheba needed to mold into the environment she was in. It's irrelevant to me whether or not David actually made the promise to Bathsheba. What's most important is seeing how the trauma of living in a perpetual conspiracy of silence molded her interactions within the family. I do not blame Bathsheba; instead, I find her to be someone who lives in the intersections of grit, resilience, and healing.

In May 2013, Chinese American researcher and scientist Angela Lee Duckworth introduced the world to the power of grit via her TED Talk. She explained that being a seventh-grade math teacher helped her understand that grit is a predictor for success. "Grit is passion and perseverance for very long-term goals," she said. "Grit is having stamina. Grit is sticking with your future, day in, day out, not just for the week, not just for the month, but for years, and working really hard to make that future a reality. Grit is living life like it's a marathon, not a sprint."[3]

To have grit is to stay steady on the goal, regardless of the obstacles. Grit is about achieving long-term results, and it exemplifies a mentality in which the ends justifies the means. To have grit is to be sandpaper. Our edges rub against the surfaces of the environments we're in—other people, institutions, or situations—and sometimes our edges are able to whittle down and smooth out the surface; other times the surface has a stronger grit than we do and we're the ones left smooth and malleable. To have grit is to recognize that you are in a place of perpetual competition, and your resolve is to outcompete the obstacles that try to wear you down. Grit empowers us to make changes that favor equity over oppressive social hierarchy. We need grit to survive those places and do the marathon-like work of creating change.

While grit is about staying dedicated to the long-term vision, resilience is about the ability to bounce back quickly. In 2016 I began my journey of learning about how childhood trauma impacts individuals and society. At that time, I was attending multiple workshops on creating trauma-informed environments for those who have experienced the traumas of immigration, community violence, poverty, and the foster care system. In every training, we focused on creating resilience for our clients. We learned how to build restorative relationships so that clients could have safe spaces to build the resilience needed for functioning in society. What I like about resilience is that it allows people to build the capacity to cope and adapt to stressful environments. What I don't like about resilience is that it expects the person to change, rather than seeking to alter the way harsh environments operate. When we center resilience too much, we create excuses for institutions and environments. Resilience without advocacy is a flatline initiative.

Bathsheba intertwines grit and resiliency. She makes her way in David's palace, surviving its challenges and achieving her long-term goal of having Solomon crowned king. We live in a society that admires and promotes the strength seen in Bathsheba and in all women who power through difficult circumstances. But I've realized that grit and resilience have their limitations; they are dependent on the ability of survivors to operate in spaces where they continually experience powerlessness. To have grit is to develop a long-term relationship with powerlessness in order to achieve a goal. The "bounce back" factor of resilience implies that the victim will continuously experience triggering or traumatic events. Both qualities are needed to help survivors navigate harmful environments, but narratives glorifying grit and resilience communicate that the only way to thrive is to remain in environments where violence is expected.

I used to hang on every word of that TED Talk. I championed building resilience and took pride in my grit. I would affirm the ways I have fought against systems of harm: *I survived so much. I made it through. I am strong.* That practice ended on a clear day when a friend and fellow abolitionist asked me a question: "Who would you be if you didn't have to fight for yourself?" I didn't know how to answer, because I didn't know who I was if I wasn't trying to defend my humanity. Those of us who grew up fighting for ourselves often lose our ability to know where the fight ends and where we begin. We become as harsh as the environments that formed us. Grit and resilience keep us alive and help us to continue fighting, but what good is it if we cannot find healing?

I believe there is goodness in what grit and resilience develop in survivors. I also think we need a space to lay our heads down and release our burdens. We need to heal. Healing is different from grit and resilience because it restores our ability to have consent and control. A healing space doesn't rely on the long-term sturdiness of grit, nor does it require resilience's ability to quickly cope and "bounce back." To heal is to discover one's power outside of the rigid systems and expectations of places that cause harm. Being in healing spaces allows us to grow into our identities, tell our stories, and shape a community that centers flourishing over productivity.

When I read through Bathsheba's story, I can't find any place where a healing space is created for her by others. Alone and imprisoned in the gilded cage of her rapist, she learns that solace happens as she gains power. Once her son Solomon is crowned king, Bathsheba rises to the position of queen mother, allowing her enough power to influence the throne of Israel. Scripture shows us that Bathsheba uses this power to have David's son Adonijah killed. I feel an odd blend of sadness and strength in Bathsheba's story. I am sad that she conformed to the carceral logic of her environment, and I am empowered to know that she was able to cause pain in the household that abused her. I am reconciling myself to this blend of sadness and strength, allowing both to exist within me. It reminds me that there is no easy route to abolition. As abolitionists, we live in the tension of knowing that, for Bathsheba, the justice being served is the only justice available to a survivor who is not in a place that centers her healing.

What I see in Bathsheba is the survivor's dilemma of not becoming as violent as the prison she is trapped in. She was pressured, powerless, disenfranchised, and violated. She grew to become honest, defensive, tender, and calculating. I mourn how Bathsheba spent most of her life in an environment that used silence as a continual torture device. I celebrate how her grit and resilience helped her survive, and I earnestly wish she had people around her or a space where she could heal.

Perhaps this is what it means to live in the legacy of Bathsheba. We who have survived so much violence deepen our grit and resilience. And we, the carriers of her legacy, reach our hands out to create the healing spaces she was never able to receive. In our tiredness and terror, we hold each other with the words that she didn't receive: *I'm here. I'm listening. I believe you. It's not your fault.*

Sitting in that online space with other Asian American women was a reminder that we live in the legacy of women who themselves were oversexualized and silenced. The role forced upon them was to remain powerless in order to sustain the wars in our Home countries and within this country we now call home. It has been years since we communed together in that healing space of women held by each other. I still remember the voice of Erna Kim Hackett announcing repeatedly, "We are Bathsheba."

We are women who have been used for the comfort and sexual satisfaction of imperialist warmongers. We are women oversexualized to sustain the fetishized mindset of manifest destiny. We are women whose pain has been silenced. We are women who have been shaped to be resilient in places where people are unwilling to recognize the harm we have been caused. We are women who are told to romanticize our grit and press forward in places of harm. We are women who die when a privileged boy emboldened with religious zeal has a bad day.

This legacy is exhausting.

My hope remains in this: we are joining together to create a community of healing that centers our voices. I am thankful for these spaces where Asian sisters speak truth and create communities that dismantle the conspiracy of silence that shrouds us. I am thankful for the strength we gain from our activist sisters abroad who are loudly resisting the atrocities of war back Home. Yes, we still carry the legacy of Bathsheba. But to carry her legacy means we are given the opportunity to create better. Unlike her, we have access to deeper community, widespread communication, and more resources. Our collective healing will shape the next generation and, in some poetic way, will give Bathsheba the grace she was never given when she was alive.

The Filipina women survived the violent atrocities done to them by imperialists have a saying, "Sa awa ng Dios," which means "through the mercy of God."[4] I take their words and cry out a prayer for all of us marked by generations of war crimes and gender violence: *Gagawin natin ito sa pamamagitan ng awa ng Diyos.*

This chapter is written in memory of the victims of the Atlanta massacre: Delaina Ashley Yaun, 33; Paul Andre Michels, 54; Xiaojie Tan, 49; Daoyou Feng, 44; Hyun Jung Grant, 51; Suncha Kim, 69; Soon Chung Park, 74; and Yong Ae Yue, 63.

Chapter Eight

Hegai and Vashti

After these things, when the anger of King Ahasuerus had abated, he remembered Vashti and what she had done and what had been decreed against her. Then the king's servants who attended him said, "Let beautiful young virgins be sought out for the king. And let the king appoint commissioners in all the provinces of his kingdom to gather all the beautiful young virgins to the harem in the citadel of Susa under custody of Hegai, the king's eunuch, who is in charge of the women; let their cosmetic treatments be given them. And let the young woman who pleases the king be queen instead of Vashti." This pleased the king, and he did so. . . .

When the turn came for Esther daughter of Abihail the uncle of Mordecai, who had adopted her as his own daughter, to go in to the king, she asked for nothing except what Hegai the king's eunuch, who had charge of the women, advised. Now Esther was admired by all who saw her. When Esther was taken to King Ahasuerus in his royal palace in the tenth month, which is the month of Tebeth, in the seventh year of his reign, the king loved Esther more than all the other women; of all the virgins she won his favor and devotion, so that he set the royal crown on her head and made her queen instead of Vashti.

—Esth. 2:1–4, 15–17

A Eunuch's Golden Shovel

"After that I will go to the king, though it is against the law,
and if I perish, I perish."

—Esth. 4:16

Boneburden is not remembering *before* exists. **After**
is a homeplace. baring hidden manifestations of captivity **that**

still hears the brethren wailing in languages barely known, **I**
would have killed myself. Silent vengeance and churning **will**.

Motivation: chilling ache in organs now **go-**
ne. Cut. Sliced. Ripped out. A dismembered penis **to**

protect aching virgin sacrifices prepared for **the**
drunkinsecure ruler. I miss Vashti. Taunting the **king**

with her free will. A blade of grass would bow before her **though**
no one knows if she is the grass or above **it.**

She placed a bangle in my hand and told me, *it* **is**
you who shall choose who protects people **against**

a kingeater, choose wisely. Her spirit, **the**
new moon steering me towards hope. I, embodied **law**.

Rage made harem home. Beauty, rape **and**
girls suffering to become housewhores—there is no **if.**

Becoming for each other what **I**
could not offer: sisters, mothers, friends, lovers. **Perish-**

ing to please crownedcaptor. A nightshade blooming girl, **I**
gave her the bangle. Chosen to unhollow hope . . . lest we **perish**.

Invisibilization

I have a confession to make: my guilty pleasure is to watch awful movie renditions of the book of Esther. I haven't seen one that is good. It's not that the story in the Hebrew Bible is bad; it's that the white Christian imagination is so awful it ruins it. If someone created a white Hollywood hegemony bingo card, I'm sure that each Esther movie would get a perfect bingo every time. There are so many elements of destruction in these movies: the brown facing, desexualization, overdramatization, monogamy, Greek-style costuming (despite this story taking place in ancient Persia), the pretty white girl who plays Hadassah/Esther, raspy voices that are a disappointment to Persian phonetics, and the weird evil twitches that most actors who play Haman the Agagite include in their creative vision of the character. I love it all. I'll sit and watch these movies with my church fan in hand as I hoop, holler, and cackle my way through each scene. I know the sole purpose of these movies was to inspire and convert, but they spark way too much microaggressive insult and laughter for me to ever take them seriously.

There's one Esther movie that I enjoy watching with limited amounts of laughter. (I still angry-laugh at the way King Ahasuerus is played by a sensitive white guy with abs, eyeliner, and a spray tan that screams, "Fire the body-bronzing artist!") I like to watch it because Hegai, one of my favorite characters in the book of Esther, is played by the late Tommy Lister Jr., also known as Deebo from *Friday*. (May he rest in power.) In one of his few scenes he stands at the harem of stolen virgins looking Black, buff, and intimidating as ever. He gives Esther key information so that she may win the heart of the king and become his queen. I use the word *heart* loosely. It's more like this: Hegai, a man who experienced genital mutilation and is enslaved to an inadequate emperor, gives details to help a trafficking victim give a man with more wives and concubines than days in the year the most unforgettable lay of his drunken life.

What I love about the book of Esther is that it is the only book in the Hebrew Bible in which God does not directly interfere. No prophet shows up. God is silent. There is no magical moment when—poof!—everything is fixed because God stepped in. God doesn't do that.

Instead, we find God in the people: in their protests, their organizing, their laments, their letters, and their resistance.

There is something so boringly heteronormative in how we approach the book of Esther. There is so much within the story if we just allow ourselves to see beyond the inadequate lenses a bigotry-based society grants us. We're taught to glorify only Esther and Mordecai's bravery, but there are many other people who bravely defied the ruler of the great Persian Empire. Hadassah wouldn't have been trafficked and transformed into Esther if it hadn't been for the self-respect and bodily autonomy displayed by Vashti. Esther wouldn't be queen without those directives from Hegai. (Let's give a round of applause for the cupbearer, allegedly Nehemiah, who kept the booze flowing just enough for the king's moods to float between cheerfulness and confusion.) Choosing to focus our attention on two characters within this book leaves out the genius of collective organizing toward liberation. I think the reason why we choose to center Esther and Mordecai is because they fit into our gender stereotypes: Mordecai as a father/uncle figure and the virgin Esther as one who models beauty, grace, and obedience to God. Everyone else remains in the background because, if we focused on them, we'd run the risk of queering God's story.

To queer a story is to combat social hierarchies and inequities to shift our focus so that we may expand beyond gender- and sex-based binaries. I think queering is important because it challenges the narratives that keep us from seeing the humanity in one another. In chapter 6, I queer-coded Jael's story to combat the gender binary. In this chapter I want to explore the queering of Hegai and Vashti to see the movement of God at work in our own lives.

King Ahasuerus deeply trusts Hegai and so chose him to oversee the care of the trafficked virgins. Hegai's relationship to the king informs my belief that he had a bond with the banished Queen Vashti. Why else would King Ahasuerus have chosen Hegai if the eunuch didn't already understand the king's sexual preferences? Hegai knew that every woman under his jurisdiction would be raped. A part of his role was making one rape victim the most delightful for the king. It's so cruel that a male victim of genital mutilation is instrumental in overseeing young victims of sex trafficking. Those who can read Esther's story and look beyond the opulence of queendom to see her as a victim of trafficking still show little empathy for Hegai, who is also a victim of sexual violence.

Eunuchs are cisgender males who have been castrated to serve a function within their government. Servants, scholars, jailers—all are roles occupied by eunuchs within Scripture. They are often treated as set decorations in God's story, but eunuchs are driving forces in doing God's work. Hegai prepared Esther to become queen. Ebed-melech the Cushite rescued the prophet Jeremiah from dying in the cistern and was rewarded by God by not being killed at the fall of Babylon (Jer. 38). The eunuch of Ethiopia is credited for introducing Christianity to northeastern Africa and thus allowing it to spread throughout the continent (Acts 8). We can't separate Hegai's identity as a eunuch from his key role in conducting God's plan to liberate the Jews from genocide.

I love that Hegai is shrouded in mystery, because it allows me the opportunity to create multiple backstories of who he is and what his motivations were. Was he forced to be a eunuch, or did he choose this life? Who were his people? Who became his people? Who loved him, and whom did he love? There is so much to inquire about Hegai and so many ways to approach his character. I find two truths of Hegai's character to be very important: Hegai chose Esther and leveraged his privilege to help her become queen; and, as a eunuch, Hegai defies the gender binary that is so very obsessed with genital function and procreation.

It's important to mention that Scripture genders Hegai with *he/him* pronouns. I'll do the same. Hegai's identity as a eunuch means he doesn't have the organs our contemporary society claims are required for maleness. Yes, I am talking about testicles. Kibble and bits. Nuts and bolt. Banger and mash. Don't believe me? Let me remind you there's a very voyeuristic and ridiculous Fox News documentary titled *The End of Men* using the image of a straight white male tanning his testicles to lament toxic masculinity's decline.[1] The patriarchal imagination is very simple: penis + testicles = man. Anything outside of the math equation is deviant and ill-fitting of their rigid gender roles. But Hegai's existence disproves that. He exists outside of the patriarchal expectation of marriage and procreation. What then becomes of our rigid understanding of gender if sex is off the table?

Hegai is a survivor of genital mutilation. It's a form of institutionalized disablement because bodily function is lost. My Catholic, evangelical, and Black Baptist upbringings all agreed that maleness is directly related to one's ability to procreate. Hegai didn't have the organs for that; did that make him any less of a man? I don't think so. Hegai was disabled by the Persian Empire. If we do not name this, then we run the risk of saying that Hegai was asexual without ever knowing his sexuality. To assume that castration is linked to asexuality is ableist and queerphobic because it disregards the reality of folks who live on the asexual spectrum. As my friend Alicia once explained to me, "Castration, regardless of how it's done, doesn't negate sexual desire. It just shifts what sexual realities are possible." Hegai has a disability that also queers the story of Esther. To deny the importance of his existence is to call into question our allegiance to sexual invisibilization and eugenics. It's an injustice how we invisibilize the characters who are necessary to the story but don't fit into the restrictive confines of complementarian heterosexuality and procreation. Kai Cheng Thom—a writer, former social worker, and pleasure activist—explains that sexual invisibilization is the perception of someone as unworthy and undeserving of erotic pleasure by the dominant culture. This cisgender heteronormative white supremacist American society regularly teaches us to sexually invisibilize people who don't fit into its standard of normal: the elderly, disabled people, queer and trans folks.[2] Invisibilizing a person is a form of dehumanization that takes part in the unjust practice that is eugenics. Eugenics is a practice of intentionally excluding people of certain identities for building a "good creation" or "master race." Hegai, who has been sexually invisibilized by way of the institutional disablement of castration, is a eugenics survivor who takes a key role in stopping Haman's pending plans for genocide of the Jews.

Hegai is a servant of the Persian Empire. He doesn't resist or try to revolutionize it. Instead, he works within the empire to make changes that end up benefiting the Jews. I often think about the power of his story. It seems that he is an obedient slave forced to do as the empire says. But Hegai makes small choices that have profound effects within Esther's story. In favoring Esther above the other trafficked women, he exercises choice. The ability to choose is not something to be taken lightly, especially for a disabled man enslaved to an empire. Hegai's favor reminds me that the practice of honoring our choice and bestowing our favor creates ripple effects that can lead us to liberation.

"We gotta be careful—protective," warns Prey Tell. "Remember this is for us, *our* community. We are not a tourist attraction. Our greatest asset is our authenticity." This scene is from season 2 episode 4 of the hit TV show *Pose*, which is about New York City's 1990s ballroom culture scene and the LGBT+ subculture of Black and Latinx communities. In this scene, Prey Tell, emcee and mentor, is meeting with three other ballroom emcees to organize the logistics of the ballroom scene. They have just finished a heart-wrenching discussion on minimizing their ballroom's "moments of silence" because too many within the community are dying from AIDS. They transition the conversation toward a lighter note, like protecting the community from the violence that comes with the hypervisibility brought by Madonna's song "Vogue" and her pending Blond Ambition tour.

Prey Tell's warning and dedication to keeping the ballroom sacred for their community is a reminder of what can happen when cultural appropriation comes for marginalized and targeted peoples. The beauty of a subculture is that it allows new realities to be fashioned; the danger of it is that once that subculture is placed on a platform to be consumed, all that's left are the dry bones left behind by culture vultures. This is indicative for all the ways the Black, non-Black persons of color, and LGBT+ cultures have built themselves up, got put on display for consumption, then became the shame and blame of American society's downfall. The house ballroom subculture, born from Black and Latinx LGBT+ folks resisting the racial discrimination of the white-favoring drag ball scene, was a means of expression and protection from the many layers of violence that targeted Black and Brown queer and trans people. It created a new reality where love was at the center for people who were denied the urgent necessity that is love, acceptance, and human connection.

A house ball was where individuals could tell their stories and use their creativity to create a montage of autobiographies for the out-casts of a cisgender heterosexual patriarchal world. Voguing—the iconic dance style of New York's house ball scene—was a living tes-tament to radical love and resistance. "Voguing is very much about telling one's story through movement," says Julian Kevon Glover, a Black queer nonbinary femme assistant professor in the depart-ment of gender, sexuality, and women's studies at Virginia Com-monwealth University. "And that for me, because of who is doing it, is very much an act of resistance to an entire world that not only tells us that our lives are devoid of meaning, but also tells us that we have nothing to contribute. It's a kind of resistance, an embodied kind of resistance, to these cultural messages. To say, 'No, I have a story to tell, and my story is going to be so convincing, that in this particular atmosphere you're going to be able to clearly understand what it is that I'm saying.'"[3] Movements toward human flourishing happen in the spaces where radical love and nuanced reality exist. It is in these places where people have the ability to define who they are and what they deserve that we find our collective liberation.

The issue is that when these cultures of resistance become objects to be consumed—appropriated as voguing was in Madonna's hit song—we lose our balance and stumble away from the freedom road. What is loved becomes what is blamed or erased. People become plot devices made to move culture along. What they truly deserve is to be known as main characters blessing us with the ingenuity that comes with radical self-love and survival.

It is through this lens that I choose to look at Hegai, a disabled social outcast whose identity is made to be an example of an empire's cruelty; yet he resists. It is through his own radical self-love that he cultivates his identity, leverages his privilege, and becomes a godfa-ther for the movement of liberating Jewish people. Hegai is more than a plot device; he is the embodiment of organizing and strategy necessary in budding liberation movements. Mordecai and Esther are important in the book of Esther, but they would not have achieved their goals if Hegai and Vashti had not first chosen to resist.

Vashti's intersection with Hegai is necessary for God's work. Queen Vashti needs to defy the king for Esther to become a liberator. The foundation of the entire book of Esther rests on Vashti's crown. King Ahasuerus holds a 180-day-long celebration for his government officials, ministers, army, nobles, and the governors of Persia's 127 provinces. Its purpose is to flaunt his wealth, to promote the well-being of the empire, and to swing some "big dick energy" around the palace. To close the ceremonious brag, the king holds a seven-day banquet in the court of the garden within his palace. This is a men-only shindig where everyone is ordered to drink without restraint. Your testosterone-filled frat-house dreams could *never*.

On the seventh day, when King Ahasuerus is slovenly unsober, he commands seven of his eunuchs to bring Vashti to the banquet in her royal crown to show the people and officials her beauty. In other words, the king wants Vashti to wear her crown and walk naked among the banquet attendees to be admired. Vashti says no. The king's embarrassment quickly turns to rage. The king's advisors tell the king to make an example of Vashti so that no other Persian wives do something so terrible as to say no. To protect the fragile ego of patriarchal men, a decree is sent far and wide declaring that all women will give honor to the Persian Empire by always saying yes to their husband's requests.

I hold Vashti in high regard as an anti-patriarchal figure who chooses to live outside of the oppressive imagination of male sexual fantasy. Scripture tells us she is beautiful and worthy of being flaunted, yet it emphasizes the importance of her saying no. Within the throes of a violent empire, Vashti delivers her no despite knowing that it will bring punishment to her. For Vashti, her bodily autonomy is more important than the king's pride and the Persian Empire's glory.

No is a full sentence. It's a whole lesson, and unfortunately, the Christian church doesn't teach it well or at all. We are taught to obey, to trust in those who have authority over us, and we're taught that saying no is blasphemy. "No" will always be a blasphemy to people who regard themselves as God. The king's rage—and the rage of his patriarchal counselors—leads to the pendulum swinging the opposite way. They institutionalize yes for their benefit, masturbating their God-complex.

There was a time when I was upset with Vashti for defying the king because I blamed her for the trafficking of innocent young virgins. I blamed Vashti for Esther's suffering. But that type of thinking was rooted in a patriarchal mind frame. As I pursued a liberative way to read Scripture, I had to confront the ways my understandings still served patriarchy. When I hold Vashti, I have to reconcile my desire to blame her for the suffering of women who have come after her. Vashti lived her truth—that her body was her own—and the violence that followed was not her fault. It was the fault of the oppressors' wrath and their unwillingness to live lives that don't worship their god complex or center their comfort.

Though Hegai and Vashti are plot devices to the story of Esther, they embody what it means to live freely in one's truth. I used to think that truth was universal in that Christianese type of way. Every time someone shared their life experience and said, "I'm speaking my truth," I would recite, "Jesus is the Truth," in my head over and over again until the next words that came out of my mouth were some form of spiritual gaslighting. I was a Christian who could recite Scripture and tell you all about Jesus, but I couldn't connect with people. No matter how well intentioned my efforts were, people could see through the facade. I am very thankful for the people who saw through this and called me into the greater work of being my authentic self and being in a community where we can connect and engage with others in ways that honor our identities. In John 14:6 Jesus calls himself "the way, the truth, and the life," then adds that no one will receive God apart from Jesus. These words became a burden to me. I thought I had to introduce everyone to Jesus. I thought I had to let them know that the only way to joy was through him. Jesus is still my center, but as I expand, so does my relationship to what centers me. What I love about Jesus as truth is that he creates space to hear people's truths. Jesus listened. He only condemned when people were abusing their privilege. He showed up for desperate and hurting people. He sat and listened to people in their joy, pain, and desperation. He wasn't afraid of hurt and didn't try to silence it with shallow, toxic positivity. Jesus loved people. His truth was being able to hold and heal other people as they sought their own understanding of truth.

My friend Rose likes to remind me that there are many forms of truth. We want truth to be objective, but it isn't. Life experiences form our perspective, and these perspectives become our personal truth. As we share our truth we allow ourselves the opportunity to expand our perspectives, engage deeply and empathetically with others, and broaden our movements toward flourishing together. It's an opportunity to move toward the curve of justice. I used to get uncomfortable when people said, "This is my truth." Now I realize that I was uncomfortable with it because I was deeply entrenched in an abusive religious system that taught me how to create barriers instead of exercising empathy. I learned that making truth subjective does not mean that it will turn us away from a deeply universal and embodied love. It draws us closer to it. My reality doesn't dictate someone else's truth, but sharing my life experience can expand their perspective if they're willing to listen with empathy. I am shifting toward this understanding of truth because it's important for us as Christians to pursue the gospel in a way that honors people's free will and capacity for consent.

This is why I love Hegai and Vashti. These characters are supposed to be plot devices who set us up for the real drama to unfurl. They defy the complementarian heteronormative norms conservative Christianity told us that we're "supposed" to follow. Their roles are supposed to be hidden and unacknowledged. But they aren't. We see how they hold their truth and give themselves consent to leverage gained privileges and disrupt the Persian Empire's violence.

Choice and consent are key. Liberative movements hang on the balance of our capacity to exercise both. As we give consent to ourselves to expand beyond the barriers of religious and institutional traumas, we are creating space for others to give consent to themselves. We cannot force our thoughts, our bodies, or our truths upon each other and call it liberative. There is no justice in the places where we can't exercise our free will and be our full selves.

Consent is a form of queering because it subverts social hierarchies and hetero-patriarchal norms. Consent gives us the tools to humanize our disabled siblings who have been sexually invisibilized and taken advantage of. When we can live freely and fully into the truthfulness of our beautifully diverse humanity, then we are able to move toward a liberative reality. The place of liberation and human flourishing is the kingdom of God—a compelling yet purely speculative vision, because we have not seen it and do not know it yet. We construct the kingdom of God more and more as we move away from the places of restriction and harm. To live fully in our identities and to love in a way that centers safety while creating fulfilling spaces for consent to exist is to do kingdom work.

Let me be clear about some things: disability is not a curse, and queerness isn't a choice. That kind of thinking is harmful and has been murderous. One person reclaiming their gender identity will save their life, and it can save the lives of many others seeking to reclaim their own. The work of reclaiming gender identity depends on using self-agency to live authentically. Liberation from oppression is incomplete if we do not keep disability justice at its center. Being able to live fully in the truth of who we are and be in communities that create space for ourselves and others to have the agency to own our truth, choose ourselves, and practice consent is a work of heaven.

Christianity is horrible with practicing choice and consent. We don't know what it is or what it feels like because we've been taught to deny it from ourselves. So many of us are taught what to do, how to think, and whom to believe. We're coerced into believing that asking questions is heretical and challenging authority is demonic. What I love about Jesus is how his work as rabbi and community organizer is predicated on the practice of consent. His conception was dependent on Mary saying yes. That's consent. When Jesus asks the disabled and chronically ill man, "Do you want to be made well?" that's consent. The demon Legion asks Jesus to put them in the pigs, and Jesus does it. That's consent. The centurion asks Jesus to heal his servant. That's consent. Sprinkled throughout the life of Jesus are acts of consent that initiate his miracles. Choice and consent precede the miracles and, most importantly for us, they are the miracle.

Consent is not an intellectual decision. It happens in our bodies. We must be able to trust our bodies and *feel* in order to begin having a practice for consent. I've been in many Christian traditions that have taught me how to manipulate my emotions toward toxic positivity instead of feeling, questioning, processing, and accepting them. My choices were not my own because I existed in a religious system that taught me my feelings are untrustworthy. Audre Lorde explains that to feel is to engage in the erotic. The erotic is not simply about sexual arousal, although sexy is a feeling and feelings are sexy. "The erotic is a measure between the beginnings of our sense of self and the chaos of our strongest feelings," writes Lorde. "It is an internal sense of satisfaction to which, once we have experienced it, we know we can aspire. For having experienced the fullness of this depth of feeling and recognizing its power, in honor and self-respect we can require no less of ourselves."[4] The erotic is feminine energy that gives power to those willing to experience it fully.

It gave Hegai the power to recognize Esther's leadership and liberative energy. Vashti was accessing her erotic energy when she denied the objectification commanded by the king. "In touch with the erotic, I become less willing to accept powerlessness, or those other supplied states of being which are not native to me, such as resignation, despair, self-effacement, depression, self-denial," Lorde says.[5] The purpose of our erotic power is to allow us to recognize what treatment is unacceptable, dismantle the systems that build that treatment, and build a new world on top of the ashes of what was dismantled. The erotic allows us the ability to feel and discern, which are two rights that have been stolen from people raised in systems of spiritual abuse. Our feelings are called carnal and demonized. Our discernment is deemed untrustworthy until an authority figure approves of it. Because we are formed to not know ourselves, we become the demons we're told to profusely pray away.

The book of Esther is a spiritual exploration of the erotic. When reading this book of the Hebrew Bible, I find myself assessing power and how it's used. Who has power? Who is wielding power? Who leverages power? Who yields power? Who is giving up their power? How is their power used? Where does their power come from? These are all questions I ask in order to discover a puzzle piece in God's design for liberation. With each question, I bring myself back to the lens of the erotic. As the power shifts throughout the story, one constant is that the two plot-device characters lay the foundation of how power can be used in a liberative way.

Hadassah becomes Esther who becomes the queen of Persia. In

this last stage she accesses the power of her erotic energy. She is a victim of Persia who has not yet grown into the power of her fully erotic self. The trafficking lair she is imprisoned in offers her beauty treatments and etiquette trainings all while using her own trauma to suppress her erotic feminine energy. Mordecai's presence is a key factor in her story because he was once the source of her discernment, but as the stakes of her story get higher, she realizes that she can no longer lean on him. She must trust herself. Self-trust is the erotic at work. It allows us to exercise choice and consent to bare our truth and dismantle the obstacles that halt us from proclaiming it.

Hegai gives Esther permission to become more than a charming sex slave. They both know she'll be raped, so he gives her pathways to practice her own agency by choosing how she will sway her rapist. (It's twisted, but no one said empowerment was a flowerbed of good times.) Queen Vashti lays the foundation of what it means to tap into the power that has made Esther a victim. Once Queen Esther claims erotic energy for herself, she ends the violence of her people by giving them consent to protect themselves. The erotic is transformative. It allows us to pour out transformative love that liberates ourselves, ends the harmful cycle of invisibilization, and creates inclusive communities. With it we learn how to say no, organize agitation, disrupt power, leverage our privilege, connect deeply with people, and help others grow more deeply into themselves. Esther is indeed the hero of the book named after her, but I think we must also create space to say that Vashti and Hegai are the heroes who laid the foundation for Queen Esther to be her fully erotic and powerful self.

Chapter Nine

Gomer

When the LORD first spoke through Hosea, the LORD said to Hosea, "Go, take for yourself a wife of prostitution and have children of prostitution, for the land commits great prostitution by forsaking the LORD." So he went and took Gomer daughter of Diblaim, and she conceived and bore him a son.

And the LORD said to him, "Name him Jezreel, for in a little while I will punish the house of Jehu for the blood of Jezreel, and I will put an end to the kingdom of the house of Israel. On that day I will break the bow of Israel in the Valley of Jezreel."

She conceived again and bore a daughter. Then the LORD said to him, "Name her Lo-ruhamah, for I will no longer have pity on the house of Israel or forgive them. But I will have pity on the house of Judah, and I will save them by the LORD their God; I will not save them by bow or by sword or by war or by horses or by horsemen."

When she had weaned Lo-ruhamah, she conceived and bore a son. Then the LORD said, "Name him Lo-ammi, for you are not my people, and I am not your God."

—Hos. 1:2–9

Hosea 3 Redacted

Part 1

The Lord said to me again, "Go, love a woman who has a lover and is an adulteress, just as the Lord loves the people of Israel, though they turn to other gods and love raisin cakes." So I bought her for fifteen shekels of silver and a homer of barley and a measure of wine. And I said to her, "You must remain as mine for many days; you shall not prostitute yourself; you shall not have intercourse with a man, nor I with you." For the Israelites shall remain many days without king or prince, without sacrifice or pillar, without ephod or teraphim. Afterward the Israelites shall return and seek the Lord their God and David their king; they shall come in awe to the Lord and to his goodness in the latter days.

Part 2

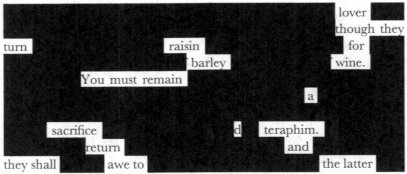

Part 3

lover
though they turn
raisin for barley wine
you must remain a
sacrificed teraphim. Return
and they shall awe
to the latter

Insecure Attachment

What I love about poetry is how it is as beautiful as it is frustrating. Poetry doesn't have to comply to form or function; it rebukes rules, releases linear thinking, exposes emotional allegiances, and celebrates the unique properties of the written word all while exploiting everyday language. Poetry is a disobedience. It is no wonder that the prophets used poetry to convey cosmic concepts and relay transformative messages to the people.

Hosea's book is a long-form series of poems made to expose how Israel's loose allegiance to the Lord has led to the colonization, exile, and harm of its people. The thread of this entire book is the metaphor of a marriage that reveals the complexity of Israel's relationship with God. The marriage in question is Hosea's marriage to Gomer, the promiscuous woman who is sexually unbound.

The thing about art is that we don't get to consume how it is received. We artists create what comes from our psyche and souls, but our creation forms into something else entirely depending on who is contemplating or consuming it. Art, in some way, is about having control and relinquishing it. I believe biblical prophecy relies so heavily on the poetic form because it allows people to engage with it from their different locations. In Hosea, we see and experience two different forms of relinquishing control: the first is Hosea's journey in releasing his control of having a sexually promiscuous wife and our journey of releasing control of how the verse is interpreted. The journey ahead is Hosea's *and ours*, and somewhere in between we'll find God in the interpretations.

Hosea wrote this poetic prophecy with a specific audience in mind: men who believed that women were property who represented the respectability of the men in their family. This is patriarchal prophetic poetry, and therefore, the metaphor on marriage is deeply rooted in control dynamics assumed to be love. One can have deep affection for what and who one controls, but that is not a place where love abides. And so we mustn't look to Hosea's book as the epic romance that it is often portrayed as.

There was once a time in my life when I fell for the romance scheme. I bought all the romance books that exemplified Hosea and

Gomer's relationship. I watched those silly little youth group movies that reenacted the summary of the story. I read the book constantly and recommended it to people. My favorite worship songs
had choice verses from Hosea. I really thought this was a book on
romantic self-sacrificing love. The reflections of Christianity that
I grew up in didn't allow me space to see Hosea's relationship to
Gomer and our relationship to God in any other way. For a frictionless Christianity to thrive, control must be the dominant narrative
of love. Hosea is seen as doting rather than abusive. Gomer is seen
as a villain rather than a victim. And God? Well, God becomes the
architect of piety and domestic violence.

I desperately want to love Scripture, but in order to do that, I must
recognize all the ways that the interpretations I received of it have
deepened my own wounds. This also means that in order to deconstruct what I knew of this story, I needed to first heal and name all
the ways that violence had formed me into believing that control was
the only way to pursue a miracle.

"I wish I could do things without doubting myself," I told my therapist
during a session in 2019. "I wish I could just stop being so insecure."

"Camille," she said with a comforting look and a tone that was
both nurturing and stern, "you're insecure because you have insecure attachment."

At that point in my life the term *insecure attachment* wasn't new to
me. I was trained in trauma-informed care and developing trauma-
informed environments. I had learned about the concept of insecure
attachment and, being the goodie-two-shoes American missionary
that I was, had absorbed it as a concept to help others but did not
think to apply it to my own life. (I was very much the chaotic person
who needed therapy and deep healing but instead ignorantly opted
to serve in Christian ministries because "Jesus needs me to serve.")

Insecure attachment is about our attachment styles. Our attachment styles are built from the beginning of our lives by our caretakers.
The ways our first caretakers respond to our cues, distress, and neces-
sities determine how we are able to "attach," or form relationships
with others. Developing our attachment style is deeply emotional,
because how we attach is determined by our first experiences of fear,

sensitivity, and safety. As we grow, our attachment patterns guide our feelings, thoughts, expectations, and our perceptions of safety. An attachment style determines your internal dialogue. For example, those who can say and firmly believe, "I am worth coming back to," will have an attachment style that is void of neglect. On the other hand, those who believe they must please people in order to receive love will have an attachment style that reflects high anxiety or disorganized affection. Understanding attachment is a difficult and multi-layered process that requires time and relationship. It isn't something that can be assumed. I had been seeing my therapist every week for months to build the intimacy and trust needed for her to explain to me that I had insecure attachment. (In other words, attachment styles aren't zodiac signs; you can't name them instantly, and the determining factors for attachment styles are deeply involved.)

There are four different types of attachment: secure, anxious-ambivalent, avoidant-insecure, and disorganized-disoriented.

I have a disorganized-disoriented attachment style. I grew up in a household where aggression and violence were constant. The relationships that I needed to be safe were not always safe. I don't think it was intentional; I now understand that my parents didn't have the capacity to give me safety in a world that was so unsafe for them. I learned to contort myself the best I could to receive love from people who didn't have the emotional capacity to extend love or who didn't want me.

I used to think I had a face people wanted to scream at. My dad, brother, classmates, basketball coaches, dance instructors, teachers—it seemed I was always on the receiving end of hard decibels. It's not the type of screaming that's simply loud; it's the type of screaming in which spit would dabble out of people's mouths, a hand would beat a lifeless surface, veins would bulge, and eyes would open wide as their skull rattled from the excess sound waves. It was the type of screaming that said, "If you don't listen to me now, I will slap you / throw a chair at you / cut you / beat you / humiliate you / disown you." It was the type of screaming where each comma, period, and exclamation point carried a shiv. Fear and humiliation were the constant companions for a daydreamer who disappointed people often and lived in a too-loud world.

I learned to cope by crouching into small spaces where the walls knew my name. I let the silence heal my eardrums. I knew they'd never tattle on my tears. There is a corner of my childhood closet that knows me. There's a crouch space next to the mini-fridge of my college dorm. I'd curl into myself and cry in the shower. The smaller the space, the better. People often talk about "taking up space," but I was a girl who was often humiliated in open space. I didn't want to take up poisoned real estate. I learned how to let the cramped and confined spaces take me. Once in the open air I stayed stuck on hypervigilance; it was my automatic setting.

The thing about growing up needing callouses is that I tried to be callous in return. I tried to serve it back. I tried to be cruel. I carried threats in my back pocket and kept colorful insults close at hand. The first rule of a close-combat fight is not to fight unless it is absolutely necessary to protect yourself. But when most of your key bonds are marked by threats and when entrusted relationships are dirtied with humiliation, *every single* interaction with anyone else feels like a thrown punch.

The small spaces that knew me held me as I taught myself it was better to run away. I had been blamed so often and so much in my life that I grew accustomed to blaming myself, proclaiming myself too toxic, and then running away because I thought I had to live holding onto the shame that should have never been mine. I didn't have the tools to fight for a relationship and pursue reconciliation, so I fled. I ghosted people, made myself busy, chose new interests, or disassociated from relationships entirely. Those of us who grew up in toxic environments become the embodiment of the spaces we grew up in. So often I see that a toxic person is a deeply wounded child living in a world that only taught them how to tend their wounds with salt.

Let's return to Hosea and Gomer and their tumultuous marriage. At the beginning of the book, God tells Hosea to marry a promiscuous woman and use her as a living metaphor for Israel's unfaithfulness (1:2). Hosea does as the Lord says and marries Gomer. It's important to see that Gomer's father is named in these same verses. Gomer, whose name means "complete," is the daughter of a man named

Diblaim (1:3), whose name is the plural form of the word *dibah*, which means "slander." In other words, she is a woman who is complete despite being intimately connected with slander. Her relationship with Hosea begins to model that with her own father. Hosea is told to marry a *zanah*, which translates as "promiscuous woman." She is a sexually active woman with a high body count, but she's not a *zonah*, which is the Hebrew word for sex worker. Gomer is in charge of her own sexuality, but she doesn't exchange sexual actions for payment. Gomer is a woman who is in control of her sexuality, and (thanks to our patriarchal English translations of the Hebrew Bible) she is slanderously portrayed as a whore.

Gomer marries Hosea, who continues the cycle of slandering her, and bears him a son. The Lord tells Hosea to name the son Jezreel as a reminder of the Lord's oncoming violence upon the house of Jehu, the kingdom of the house of Israel, and for the destruction that will happen upon the bow of Israel in the valley of Jezreel (1:4). To put it plainly, Gomer's first son is named, "You're going to get the beating you deserve." Gomer gives birth to a second child, a daughter, whom Hosea names Lo-ruhamah, which means, "You will receive no mercy." Despite the awful name her husband has given the child, Gomer does not revoke mercy or love from her. Scripture says that she nurses her second child until a third child is conceived. Gomer carries Lo-ruhamah and nurtures her with life-giving milk. To nurse a child is to use one's own body as a vessel for nourishment. There are beautiful depictions of nursing that make it sound poetic and beautiful—but it's a lot more than that. Nursing takes a strain on one's mental health and bodily resources. It's a painful and emotional journey to help a baby latch on and remain able to continue feeding. Despite its pain, nursing deepens our biological capacity for love. As the baby latches on and feeds, the nursing body releases oxytocin (the "happy hormone") and prolactin (the "love hormone") to help the mother feel relaxed, calm, and ready to care for her baby.[1] There is much sacrifice and tenderness in nursing a child. To do so is to love deeply. Biblical scholar Wil Gafney explains: "And there it is, the place where I see God's promiscuously extravagant love in the text, not in Hosea's words or even God's, but in Gomer holding to her breast that baby girl who had to go through the world with a label on her saying she would be bereft

154   *The Hero and the Whore*

of maternal love, pity, or compassion the same way Gomer has had to go through [the] world of the text and its interpreters with the label whore hanging over her head. Gomer persisted in loving that child no matter who said otherwise."[2] Their third child was a son that Hosea named Lo-ammi. His name means, "You are not my people, and I am not your God" (1:8). Hosea gives their children names that fate them for desolation and isolation. Yet Gomer, a complete woman who has lived life under scrutiny and slander, loves each of her children deeply and nurtures each of them until they are able to stand and feed on their own.

Our attachment styles are created as our brains make emotional connections about our caretakers. The brain *depends* on social inter-action to influence the ways one's nervous system develops; it is also hardwired to *expect* certain signals—eye contact, touch, voice tonal-ity, diction, and interactions—to stimulate our social responses. The small details we know of Hosea within his family show how he is accusatory and slanderous, and how his perceptions of power roles are more important to him than the relationships he must nurture. Hosea has a wife and three children that he uses as symbols, but he doesn't share connection with them.

This marriage metaphor leaves the realm of complicated rela-tionship and enters a more problematic place. Hosea represents the patriarchal male who believes he *deserves* to be loved and respected by his wife. But does he give her the same care and attention?

Nope.

Though he marries Gomer, he continually slanders her by refer-ring to her by her list of sexual lovers, and he gives his children awful names and turns them into living metaphors of doom. Hosea's poetry consistently reveals the insecurity he has of upholding "proper" power relationships within their marriage. Because his marriage doesn't reflect the way things should be, he is forcing them into a mold that will fit the norms. In doing so, Hosea shows his true beliefs and intentions. Their household is better defined by shame and con-trol than by connection and care. Gomer, filled with blame for things she shouldn't own, flees.

I understand that Hosea's marriage metaphor was meant to shock the men of Israel into returning to their faithfulness in God. This book was written a couple millennia and a few centuries before I was born, so I'm aware that the dynamics of and outlook on relationships have changed. I don't assume that we twenty-first-century folks must live as though we operate under the same rules of occupied Israel in the eighth century BCE. Societies evolve, we deepen our capacities for compassion, and our language transforms so that we may all grow. (Or at least, that's what *should* happen.) Hosea's poetic metaphor on marriage is an outdated and destructive perspective, intended to control others. Yet I seek the same God Hosea proclaims. What do we do when the metaphor in use is also the metaphor that mirrors our abuse? What happens when I am told that my "right relationship" with God is meant to model my own anxious and disorganized attachment with my own father?

I seek new metaphors.

"YOU WHORE! YOU WHORE! YOU WHORE!"

My father stormed about the house calling me a whore because I wanted to hang out with my friends. I was seventeen, and most of my friends were guys who were into hip-hop and breakdancing. My mom said it was OK to hang out with them, but to make sure I was home long before the streetlights came on. Somehow my dad found out I had spent an afternoon with mostly guys, which triggered his tirade. He screamed at me. I cried. My father made his assumptions and flung his accusations at his one and only daughter.

My mother interceded and told him she had said it was OK. She yelled back at him to redirect his anger. She put her body between us as I lay in a fetal position on the floor. I cried, blamed myself, and blanketed myself with shame for wanting to have friends.

Just a month prior to this incident, my mom had opened up to me about a time in her childhood when my grandfather assumed she had a boyfriend and nearly beat her to death. Her brothers had to intervene and remove his body from hers to stop him.

My mom looked me in the eye as my dad calmed down and left the room. The damage was done. As she and I stared at each other, I saw her face colored with sadness and exhaustion and a small, strange spark telling me she was able to do for her child what she couldn't do for herself. As I stared into my mother's eyes, I felt a burden that lived beyond my own life and is passed down through generations.

Research on the brain shows that children have neural pathways that enable them to feel a little of what a parent is feeling when eye contact is made. Deborah Gray explains: "If the parent is frightened or remembering trauma, children will respond with the mixed strategies of freezing, avoidance, disorientation, and anger when they are around their parent. They will not want to connect with their parent's state of mind. It is too overwhelming to feel their parents' feelings."[3]

All my favorite people have daddy issues. It is because of this intriguing coincidence that I am drawn to Gomer and her children. In Hosea 2:2–3, the prophet accuses Gomer of adultery and brings the children into the situation:

> Plead with your mother, plead—
>   for she is not my wife,
>   and I am not her husband—
> that she put away her prostitution from her face
>   and her adultery from between her breasts,
> or I will strip her naked
>   and expose her as in the day she was born
> and make her like a wilderness
>   and turn her into a parched land
>   and kill her with thirst.

Hosea is telling their children that their mom has other lovers and that because of this she deserves violent punishment. (The law of Israel states that a married woman who commits adultery would either be stoned to death or beaten.) Hosea has told his children—whom he named unlovable, unredeemable, and deserving of violence—to collect their mother before he beats her to death for not upholding the power dynamics fitting a "proper" Israelite marriage.

But why did Gomer flee? If she is not a prostitute and is instead a sexually promiscuous woman, why would she leave a marriage that offered her security and sanctuary within society?

I once met with a woman (I'll call her Tracy) who had to flee her home because of domestic violence. Tracy had little access to resources and few people who supported her. Her own parents and siblings told her to stay in the relationship. Tracy knew she could not stay with her abuser, so she saved up what money she had and tried to flee with her children. But her abuser was manipulative and told her that he would kill her if she took the children. So she fled alone and wept because she couldn't bring her babies to safety with her. It took years of legal battles and navigating through life as a domestic abuse survivor, but she was able to get her children back and keep them away from her abuser. Tracy is now a middle-aged woman, and her children are adults with their own families. When I ask her about her decisions, she tells me she has no regrets. "It was hard to leave," she said, "but it was either that or stay and let myself die."

It's hard for me to read Hosea's poetry and not assume that he was an abuser who cared more about his power, piety, and reputation than his own family. What if Gomer's promiscuity was the only way she knew how to respond to her husband's abuse? I am a woman healing from the complex PTSD that came with living in a violent household. I feel heartbroken as I wonder about the pain their children felt as they looked into the eyes of the mother who loved them even though their father had named them as unlovable.

The unfortunate reality of this world is that we cannot absolve ourselves from power dynamics. There will always be someone who holds power and another person who is obedient to it. Teachers have power, parents have power, husbands have power; each example is a metaphor used to describe the complicated relationship we have with God. We can read Hosea's book with eyes of disgust and shock, but we cannot read it and assume the best course of action is to remove power dynamics in relationship. It's just not reasonable. In my own life, some of the hardest healing work that I can do is to disassociate power from abuse. I cannot hate power because it, too, is a tool for flourishing. What's most important is how I use that power to bring others to flourishing.

What I am instead learning is that a metaphor on the complexities of marriage is a metaphor rooted in control dynamics, and what lies deep within the prophetic poetic form is a lesson on how our relationships and attachment styles inform our spirituality.

As his book continues, Hosea likens himself to God and talks about how his wife has abandoned him in the same way Israel has

abandoned God (4:1–11). Hosea seeks to punish Gomer with destruction and humiliation, which is the same way the nation of Israel has
been punished by God. Then God pivots, declaring that God will not
punish the nation as it deserves but instead will deal with Israel com-
passionately (11:8–9), despite still holding up the scorecard of wrongs
and God's vast history of being a provider for sinful people (12:9–14).

What I find most interesting is how the marriage metaphor is
replaced with a parenting metaphor. In chapter 13 God goes from
jilted lover to scorned mother:

> Yet I have been the LORD your God
>> ever since the land of Egypt;
> you know no God but me,
>> and besides me there is no savior.
> It was I who fed you in the wilderness,
>> in the land of drought.
> When I fed them, they were satisfied;
>> they were satisfied, and their heart was proud;
>> therefore they forgot me.
> So I will become like a lion to them;
>> like a leopard I will lurk beside the way.
> I will fall upon them like a bear robbed of her cubs
>> and will tear open the covering of their heart;
> there I will devour them like a lion,
>> as a wild animal would mangle them. (13:4–8)

God talks of nurturing the young nation of Israel who was newly
freed from Pharoah's grip. God fed Israel beyond satisfaction. Here
God laments being forgotten as the Israelites received abundance:
"They were satisfied, and their heart was proud" (13:6). Responding
from hurt, God shifts the metaphorical imagery to predatory animals—lions, leopards, and bears—to reveal a complicated dynamic
of harm, protection, and control disguised as care. God becomes like
a lion and a leopard who will lurk beside Israel to keep the nation in
line. God will take on the persona of a fierce and enraged Syrian bear
attacking the nation of Israel, who removed her whelps from her
grasp. Then God will become like a lion ready to rip out and devour

the heart of a disobedient nation. The metaphors expose Hosea's penchant for abusing those he has power over.

Years ago, a person once told me that the first prophetic word we hear is often for ourselves. I think this same advice applies to Hosea. God will lurk near Hosea if he hurts his family. God, a mother bear, will attack Hosea for hurting God's children (namely, Gomer and the children she bore). God is a lion ready to rip out and devour Hosea's heart because Hosea's abuse is disobedience to God's will. Reading these texts makes me wonder if that prophet misunderstood that the prophecy was for himself. I believe God is a loving and kind advocate for the powerless. I refuse to believe Hosea's narration of God is a reliable source, because there is no love in abuse. Hosea cannot love that which he lords over. In the same way, God shows that a metaphor built on a manipulated form of romance within a complex marriage is insufficient for redemption. It is not God's identity as a husband that redeems Israel. I am drawn to God's description of being a mother bear, ready to attack the man who attacks and slanders his wife and children. I hold tight to this description of Mother God, intervening and pursuing a securely attached relationship with her children despite violence and harm.

This is not to say that we should only look to our mothers as the metaphor for our relationship with God—because there are some awful mothers in the world. Being a parent doesn't automatically launch someone into the atmosphere of righteousness. This is why it's so important that we reparent ourselves. Many of us survivors of domestic violence must become our own mothers, fathers, and caretakers of the inner child that lives within us in order to know the complexity of our relationship with a God who wants to tenderly build a secure attachment to us.

The core of the book of Hosea is attachment. There are more people in the world with attachment styles marked by insecurity and anxiety. It would be a disservice to our spirituality to assign the complexity of our relationship with God to Hosea's complicated marriage that has overt tones of abuse. It would be downright devastating to assert that this relationship is the peak example of love. Instead of looking to specific relationships to define who God is to us, let us center how we heal our various attachment styles in order to know God more fully.

Hosea saw relationship as function, but God uses relationships as medicine.

We American Christians do not live in the same situation as Hosea. In fact, it is because of the religiosity of our nation that other countries are forced into the similar abusive patterns of violence, slander, conquest, and exile that Israel knew in Hosea's lifetime. His understanding of God should not inform our own. Instead, we must ask ourselves how we can distort our relational power dynamics and the unintentional harm that is caused by our loyalty to those power dynamics.

I grew up in the "Jesus is my homeboy" era of Y2K evangelicalism. We'd wear shirts and baseball caps with the logo and talk about how Christianity "is not a religion; it's a relationship." Yet evangelical Christianity is dependent on turning relationships into transactions. It centers relationships with unbelievers as opportunities to create conversions. The purpose of marriage is to be a marker of holiness over happiness. (This is from a Christian marriage book I was required to read during my premarital counseling.) The role of parenting is to raise the next generation of Christian leaders. The role of friendships with other Christians is to edify one another, but if someone leaves (or flees) the faith, then their excommunication from the community they were dependent on is justifiable. More often than not, Christian relationships are built on the framework of insecure, anxious, and disorganized attachment styles created from the fear of failure and abandonment. And yet there is a proclamation that perfect love casts out fear (1 John 4:18). It is hard for me to believe that the iterations of modern-day Christianity will provide the love necessary to heal the attachment styles it created from social anxiety and fearmongering.

I have a friend (I'll call her Callie) who fled an abusive evangelical church. She spent ten years of her life dedicated to its ministries, serving its youth, and becoming so incredibly disembodied that she couldn't associate the physical pain she felt with its true cause—being boxed into a repressive spirituality. Callie told me of a time

when her spiritual mentor impressed the abuse-supporting interpretations of Hosea upon her. She would continually hear messages
that repressing her sexuality and reinforcing body shame was the
only path toward the Lord. She'd confess her sins and spiral further down into disembodiment. After leaving her church, going to
therapy, and joining a supportive community, she was able to heal
from the traumas she experienced inside and outside of the church.
As she learned how to tend to her own needs and care for her body,
she realized she couldn't continue using this framework of abuse
and remain in relationship with God. As Callie healed from childhood traumas, racism, sexism, and spiritual abuse, her relationship
with God expanded.

It was friendship that taught me how to know God deeply. Once
my husband and I left the evangelical church we had attended and
the evangelical organizations we were affiliated with, we lost the
majority of our friendships. It broke our hearts. Together we had
to learn how to be friends to one another and how to make new
friends. (Making adult friendships is really hard!) But this also created
the space for us to build relationships that didn't rely on the transactional framework that evangelical Christianity had given us. We
made friendships based on mutuality and care instead of evangelical
duty. We couldn't gaslight or Bible thump our way into a healthy
marriage or into secure relationships with others. Instead, we had
to recognize that healing attachment in friendships requires us to be
present in accountability and hurt. This meant inviting ourselves on
a journey to discover all the ways we had experienced lovelessness
and relational insecurity so that we could build deeper bonds with
ourselves, our friends, and the new communities we were building.
For me, a child of anxious and disorganized attachment prone to
blaming myself and running away from the shame of lovelessness, it
also meant that I had to feel pain in friendship. "Acceptance of pain
is part of loving practice," writes bell hooks. "It enables us to dis-
tinguish constructive suffering from self-indulgent hurt. When love's
promise has never been fulfilled in our lives, it is perhaps the most
difficult practice of love to trust that the passage through the painful abyss leads to paradise."[4] This is not the pain of the control and
abuse we see in Hosea's relationship to his family, but the pain of

journeying through accountability and connection in order to heal insecure forms of attachment.

A theme throughout the book of Hosea is forgiveness. It is necessary in relationship, but we have to be wary of how people use forgiveness to manipulate people instead of helping them heal. If Hosea does not recognize himself as an abuser, then his forgiveness toward Gomer is a manipulative tactic used to force her back into the same power dynamic that harmed her. My relationship with my father is painful, but it is still a relationship that deserves repair and forgiveness. It took years for me to forgive my father for all the ways he hurt us, but in order to forgive him I had to stop operating in the Christian mindset that told me to forgive immediately. I had to know that my capacity to forgive was a highly valuable gift rather than a spiritual obligation. As bell hooks writes:

> A useful gift all love's practitioners can give is the offering of forgiveness. It not only allows us to move away from blame, from seeing others as the cause of our sustained lovelessness, but it enables us to experience agency, to know we can be responsible for giving and finding love. We need not blame others for feelings of lack, for we know how to attend to them. We know how to give ourselves love and recognize the love that is all around us.[5]

I've had a lot of people tell me to forgive my dad. They have told me that I wouldn't be a good Christian if I couldn't forgive him. This pressure has been just as hurtful as the hurt I received in my childhood. I knew I had to forgive him, but I also knew that I needed my own time and space to find myself valuable enough to extend the gift of forgiveness to the one who deeply hurt me. In order to know my forgiveness as a gift instead of an obligation, I had to be in relationship with people who could love me into understanding that I am valuable and that—by extension—the forgiveness I gave was equally valuable.

My Aunt Ernestine is my dad's sister and one of my dearest relationships. She was the first person that I spoke to within our family about growing up in an abusive household. I was thirty-one years old when I told her. Instead of pushing me to forgive him, she said,

"I don't care if it's your dad, your mom, or whoever it is. No one is allowed to treat my niece like that." She centered her attention on caring for me and letting me know how much she loves me. She sent daily text messages, phone calls, and an occasional gift for my kids. Her consistency and love helped me begin to believe that I was worthy of receiving love without having to contort or perform for it. When I became overwhelmed and ghosted her, she would still send her texts every day and wait for me to call her on the phone, when she would respond with a joyful, "It's good to hear your voice! How's my niece?"

The safety I gained in my relationship with my Aunt Ernestine gave me the foundation to heal my own insecure attachment. Her love modeled what it looks like for me to build relationships centered on safety and security.

The lasting relationships and bonds that Black women make with one another is the metaphor that I use to describe my relationship with God. Black girls and Black women have historically been used as objects for abuse, torture, and deathmongering. We live in a society so rooted in misogynoir that it would sooner shame and accuse a Black woman for being herself rather than recognize the ways it pledges allegiance to the many and multilayered forms of violence we experience. Forty-five percent of Black women have experienced intimate partner violence in the forms of physical harm, sexual abuse, and stalking, and a staggering 53 percent of Black adult female homicide victims are the product of intimate partner violence. Black women are more likely to be victims of intimate partner homicide.[6] The healing relationships between Black women are holy because we choose our blessed identities as Black women in a society that favors one's proximity to white womanhood. Black women in healthy relationship with one another is an act of resistance to this society that tells us we should expect to be hated.

The work of Marisa G. Franco helped me understand the role that nontransactional friendships make in healing our attachment styles. Reading her book *Platonic* was my journey through understanding the healing power of relationship and community. Black women heal through friendships built on mutuality and care—two things not offered to us by society. Franco writes, "We choose our friends, which allows us to surround ourselves with people who root for us, get us, and delight in our joy. There's no looming vow, formal ritual, or genetic similarity to retain us in friendship's open palms. Through friendship, we can self-select into some of the most affirming, safe, and sacred relationships of our lives, not because of pressures from society to do so, but because we elect to do so."[7]

I won't be able to love the book of Hosea in the same way that I did when I was unaware of my complex PTSD and insecure attachment styles. But what this book has given me is a liberated way to own a complicated metaphor and find myself in it. Like Gomer, I have been sexually active, slandered, and abused. Like Gomer, I have been a nurturing presence and fled the environments that have done me wrong. And like Gomer, I have shifted the narrative of dominance as righteousness to seek a God more invested in healing attachment styles.

There is no last destination for healing. When we heal, we enter a cycle of continuance in which we continually recognize the ways that our toxic environments built our toxic traits. But that does not mean we are unlovable or deserve neglect or further abuse. Hosea writes about how he retrieves his wife and brings her back to their home. I wonder if he becomes a better husband who offers mutuality and care for her, or if this ending is a tragedy she endures. What I do know is that the book's metaphor doesn't serve us in the way the poetic prophet intended. We can find ourselves in the metaphor and use it as a launching point to pursue something better.

We don't have to associate God with abuse. Even God took Hosea's manipulative marriage metaphor to teach him that redemption relies on agitating unfit power dynamics for mutuality to thrive and insecure attachment styles to be healed.

Our spirituality can be nourished by how we move toward healthy relationships founded on mutuality, safety, and care. The question stops being, "How do we live to please God?" and becomes, "How can we heal our insecure attachments in healthy relationships *so that* we will know God's love?"

Chapter Ten

Salome

At that time Herod the ruler heard reports about Jesus, and
he said to his servants, "This is John the Baptist; he has been
raised from the dead, and for this reason these powers are
at work in him." For Herod had arrested John, bound him,
and put him in prison on account of Herodias, his brother
Philip's wife, because John had been telling him, "It is not
lawful for you to have her." Though Herod wanted to put
him to death, he feared the crowd, because they regarded
him as a prophet. But when Herod's birthday came, the
daughter of Herodias danced before the company, and she
pleased Herod so much that he promised on oath to grant
her whatever she might ask. Prompted by her mother, she
said, "Give me the head of John the Baptist here on a platter." The king was grieved, yet out of regard for his oaths
and for the guests, he commanded it to be given; he sent and
had John beheaded in the prison. His head was brought on
a platter and given to the girl, who brought it to her mother.
                                            —Matt. 14:1–11

Before She Danced, a hay(na)ku

Mother
wraps arms
around my waist

"You
look beautiful.
He'll be pleased."

She
scans my
breasts, blessing God

"we
women learn
our strengths early"

her
hands possessively
claw my hips

Revolt
looms outside
I must dance

Mother,
scandal's center,
Birthed her weapon

I'm
the quiet
in this storm

He,
its devastation.
Call him Daddy

Tonight
I dance
for military libido

StepFatherKing
will celebrate
on my body

Adultification

Every chapter is difficult to write, but this one breaks my heart.

This chapter is for the ones who were hurt when they were children forming brain synapses that would determine their understanding of this harsh world, for the vulnerable and the ones who built barbed wires to stop crying. To you, sweet melanin chocolate drop, who deserves better. And to the one carrying scars of a violated youth, this is for the child inside of you. This is for the ones who were targeted, chosen, groomed, trafficked, and singled out. This is for the ones who didn't know their story is necessary. This is for the ones who deserved a better childhood, whose brains are just now making connections and doing the exhausting work of rewiring themselves for a brighter world. This is for the ones who received disruption when they deserved connection. I am thinking of you as I write this. I am thinking of the things that couldn't be said and of each misinterpreted cry for help. Mostly, I am thinking of how we have done all we can to survive for so long. The weight has become so normal that we don't know what life could be without it. There are days when I don't know if I'm allowed to call this survival. It's life, and life has shown how little it cares for little girls and little boys and little gender-expansive children.

Know this: you deserve everything you were never able to receive.

There is a girl in the Bible who danced beautifully. Elaborately dressed, she gave a performance so stunning it would be known throughout history. This girl's dance was so incredible that it altered the course of history. She was a world changer. With her grace and her presence, she put on a performance that brought a room of leaders and warriors to its knees and merited deep applause. It is said that she danced so well that it earned her the coveted prize of a king's favor. With glee in his eyes and the pads of his hands warmed from rigorous applause, he promised to grant her whatever her heart desired.

It is unknown what the girl truly desired, because she didn't ask for it. I daresay she truly wanted her mother's love, because the girl forfeited her choice and requested what her mother the queen commanded of her. *I want you to give me at once the head of John the Baptist on a platter,* she said. The girl's mother had an agenda. She wanted to silence a man who had outspokenly condemned her newly formed marriage with the king. She knew the king and his confidants would love his stepdaughter's dance. She, knowing her daughter desperately wanted to please her, positioned her daughter to fulfill her desire. The mother, who was being characterized as an adulterer and powermonger, had to protect her reputation. In her eyes, the reputation and might of the kingdom depended on silencing the naysayer with a platform. Instead of calling for the religious zealot's demise herself, she asked her child to request John's state-sanctioned murder. Though it saddened the king to do this, he fulfilled his stepdaughter's wish. After all, the dance was very impressive. When the girl received the head of the imprisoned man she did not squirm, flinch, or cry. She gave the bodyless form to her mother and watched as the woman she so desperately wanted approval from celebrated this victory (Mark 6:21–28).

I think John the Baptist was a religious man. I regard him more as a prerevolutionary organizing the colonized people of Israel to never settle for the standard of living given to them by the Roman Empire. In baptizing the people in the Jordan River, he mobilized them into a movement of spiritual activism. That is, baptism was the induction into a person being connected with the highest power (God) to engage in the daily and active work of dismantling systems of oppression. What I love about baptism is that it's a symbolic commitment we make to do our best to abolish systems of harm that happen in our society and the forms of harm we do to ourselves. John the Baptist was an organizer, prophet, and revolutionary. To murder him outright could cause an uprising. To justify his state-sanctioned murder, there needed to be a complication. That complication was a prepubescent girl—or, rather, her body. For John to die, Salome's prepubescent body was objectified by her mother and paraded in front of her stepfather and his colleagues.

There are some uncomfortable dynamics here: a prepubescent female body, a conniving mother who objectifies her daughter, a drunk and horny incestuous stepfather surrounded by his equally drunk and horny military men. But in the telling of the story, the first detail is overlooked. Salome's body is ignored not because it is unimportant but because the storyteller wants the shock to be solely focused on John's murder. The story, instead, is told like a math equation:

> Salome danced
> + King Herod was impressed
> + Queen Herodias made the request
> = John dead.

My heart breaks for Salome, for she is a daughter who is used as a pawn by her mother and placed in a family with a predatory step-father. What is further complicated about Salome is that paintings of her do not portray her as a prepubescent girl, as the Greek term *korasion* indicates, but rather as a fully formed woman. She is adorned in jewelry as she dances, her stomach and (sometimes) breasts exposed; sometimes her back is in a variation of *combre* to accentuate curves, and her arms are extended, not simply to reach but to reveal. She is femme fatale embodied. As I look through these paintings of Salome made by male and female artists such as Italian baroque painter Artemisia Gentileschi (1615), French symbolist Gustave Moreau (1876), French salon painter Georges Rochegrosse (1887), German impressionist Lovis Corinth (1900), and Austrian symbolist Gustav Klimt (1909), I see a seductress using her bare form to achieve her mother's goal. I must remind myself she's supposed to be a prepubescent girl.

It's important to recognize that every painter I've named is European. Every artwork they've created comes from a Christo-European imagination. While Christianity is not a religion that started in Europe, it is the Europeans who co-opted it into a religion of privilege and power and eventually categorized themselves into the structure of whiteness so that the system of white supremacy can exist. It is white supremacy that inspires a very important detail in these depictions of Salome's dance: orientalism. This form of violence is as pervasive and destructive as anti-Blackness and anti-Indigeneity. But it is often overlooked because orientalism presents itself as a figment of wonder instead of a violent ethos of the white imagination. Orientalism is a fantasy of the Western imagination that objectifies and oversexualizes peoples of Asia, deeming them "unusual," "exotic," and "other." While all parts of orientalism are problematic, it is the last one—the othering—that is distressful. People who establish themselves as the moral authority give themselves the power to otherize an entire continent of diverse and complex identities. Thus, the oversexualized depictions of the child-body of Salome is a working of white European supremacy done to hypersexualize and villainize western Asia in order to establish its Christo-European mythos as the moral center. It doesn't matter that John is a descendant of the same region of western Asia as Salome. As a proto-Christian, John gets racialized as white in the European imagination, while Salome's body is barbarically unsheathed in order to orientalize, and thus villainize, her.

There is another painting of Salome that has caught my eye. It is by French painter Henri Regnault. It is a stunning piece of bright golden hues created in 1870 and named after our dancing victim/villain. However, Salome is not dancing. She is clothed. She has one shoulder exposed, an elbow pointed out as her hand sits on her hip. Her bare ankles are crossed, and the high arch of her dancer's foot is on full display. On her lap is a silver platter, without John. Instead, her hand is on the platter and holding a dagger. Her clothing is draped around her as she sits in a satisfied posture with an accomplished smile, childlike blush, and disheveled hair. She is sexual and deadly, and the golden hues surrounding her evoke a complex mix of happiness, awe, and caution. The yellow she is engulfed in was once the color used by medieval painters to single out Judas Iscariot the betrayer. But in Regnault's depiction, Salome's yellow is sartorial. (After the debut of his painting, yellow became the "it color" worn by women throughout France.) In *Salome*, femininity and violence are unmistakably intriguing.

What interests me most about this piece is that Regnault originally wanted to make it a portrait of an African woman (with an Italian woman as the model). For whatever reasons, he decided not to and chose to have elements of Africa strewn throughout the painting in order to solidify Salome as a seductress: a leopard-skin rug atop a tribal carpet, a Moroccan chest of drawers. This painting was revealed a mere fifty-five years after the death of the Khoekhoe woman who became the sexualized Black Venus of the white imagination. Regnault's *Salome* was not a figment of blackface, but for her to be villainized as the hypersexualized femme fatale she had to have elements of Africa surrounding her.

What these depictions of European art teach me is that in order for children to lose the frailty of innocence they must be set apart from whiteness. They must be othered. That happens in these cases through the two-part process of orientalization and being associated with Blackness. Once children are othered, they can no longer bear the childhood markers of innocence. Being prepubescent doesn't matter because they don't *look* young. No matter what age they are, they become adults. This process is called adultification.

To adultify is to create a bias that deems a child as less innocent and more criminal. I've heard some people say that adultification is based on looks—that a child who *looks* more physically mature will become adultified. That's one part of it. To adultify is also to assume that one type of identity is the moral authority and that those whose identities exist in contrast to that one type are presumed to be so deviant that they do not deserve the care and attention they would otherwise need. In the case of our society, it is whiteness that believes itself to hold moral authority. Nonwhite children—specifically Black, Indigenous, Pacific Islander, and brown-skinned Latinx and brown-skinned Asian children—become adultified in a white-supremacist society. And while this is the reality for children with more melanin, we must narrow our focus in order to see how adultification has specifically harmed white supremacy's intended victim: Black girls.

White conservative and evangelical Christians throw around accusations of how children are being sexually "groomed" by predators—namely the LGBT+ community, drag performers, and others who don't share their same political values, all in the name of "protecting innocent children." They prop themselves up as the moral authority—vigilantes set to rid the world of groomers so that they can provide safety and protection for children. But how often do they think of protecting Black girls? They surely are silent on this topic. Black girls experience harm more than children of other racial and gender identities. White conservative and evangelical Christians would rather blame Black girls for their wounds. A 2007 study of reported child sexual abuse survivors conducted by the US Office of Administration for Children, Youth and Families revealed that in 2005–2006 the number of Black children who were sexual abuse survivors was nearly twice the number of white or Latinx children.[1] The 2010 National Incidence Study of Child Abuse and Neglect revealed that Black children experience maltreatment at twice the rate of white children.[2] Ten years later the US Department of Health and Human Services and the Administration for Children and Families surveyed child abuse rates in the United States by race and ethnicity of victims. Black children were found to still experience child abuse at nearly double the rate of white and Latinx children.[3]

Harm done to Black children is doubled down with more policing. Their bodies, behavior, and beliefs about themselves are heavily policed. To police people means using accusations, manipulation, and physical harm to control, regulate, or perpetuate a punitive system to keep those persons in line. If the violence of policing doesn't work, their entire existence is discarded. Black children make up one of the largest percentages of missing children within the United States despite being a smaller ethnic demographic. When Black children disappear, their stories are deemed unimportant, and like Salome, they fade into the background. There is no media attention for the violated Black child in a world that hardly recognizes their humanity. Black children deserve bandages and tenderness; instead they receive shackles, lashings, policing, isolation, and the torturous lie that this is their fate. Assess the standard of care Black children receive and you'll find that the bar is in hell.

Let me speak plainly of hell: it is a religious construct architected into a culture of torture. I have spent my entire life fearing hell only to now realize that I already live in a place far worse than it. Hell as the place of endless weeping and gnashing of teeth persistently exists, but at least in hell someone will hear our pain. In this tragic reality, we are expected to keep silent and complicit.

Salome's hell was constructed by a manipulative mother ruthlessly protecting her scandalous marriage, alpha-male military leaders licking their lips at her twirl, and a stepfather who happily watched his prey shake her prepubescent hips. She is a violated child presented as an adult. She is exotified and blamed. We find her still seeking to please the mother who placed her in harm's way. There is no safety for Salome. She is still a child, intimately acquainted with what it means to be an object before being a person.

Like Salome, Black children dance on the razor-thin margins of humanity bestowed to them by this society. Black children are objectified, othered, exotified, and told that their scars could be avoided if only their behavior changed. But what is the purpose of good behavior in a murderous ecosystem? Whom does it appease? Whom does it care for? Certainly not the victims. Violence doesn't end with punitive discipline. Violence *is* the punitive discipline. The narrative surrounding the development of the Black child is centered on the act of *stopping* rather than caring. Stop the Black child from having sex. Stop the Black child from being too sexy. Stop the Black child from dressing provocatively. Stop the Black child from hanging out with those people. Stop the Black child from misbehaving. Stop the Black child from failing. Stop the Black child from being violent. Stop the Black child. Stop. Stop. Stop.

Black children are victims who are blamed at every angle of their existence.

There is nothing viler than blaming children for the harm they've encountered. Cycles of violence stay spinning because people are unwilling to dismantle the culture that creates them. The existence of sexual violence is dependent on a culture that grants permission to perpetrators. To understand the sexual violence done to Black children, we must deconstruct the culture that made their harm permissible.

A child's hell is constructed by the narratives we perpetuate.

In 2010 I had the privilege of watching Anna Deavere Smith perform a scene from her recently debuted play about health care and the body entitled *Let Me Down Easy*. Using her talents as a playwright-documentarian, she crafted this work of theatrical art by interviewing more than 300 people on three different continents. When performing this one-woman show, she did more than act—she conjured the people she spoke with. Her posture shifted, her tonality transformed.

I sat in the audience simply amazed. But there was one scene that broke me. Smith embodied a physician recounting the time she was a medical student at Charity Hospital, a public hospital in New Orleans. In this scene, the physician was talking about the days she had worked alongside a resident physician in that overpacked, overwhelmed, and undersupported hospital in post-Katrina New Orleans:

> One night when we were on call—a young woman came with pelvic inflammatory disease. So we were called to the emergency room. And it's tremendously painful to be examined when you have fulminant pelvic inflammatory disease. And she was thirteen. She was there with an aunt. But her aunt was not in the room. In fact, I think—I think if I remember right this guy [i.e., the doctor] made her aunt *leave* the room. And he did a pelvic exam on her. I want to get it right *(slight pause)*. He said, "What's your problem? *(pause)* Don't tell me that you haven't had something *bigger* than these two fingers up there, if you got this to begin with."[4]

I remember the awe I felt at Smith's ability to have written and performed the scene while also holding the sorrow of the story she told through her art. It was real. That doctor was real. That thirteen-year-old girl was real. And the things he said, the assumptions he made, were all too real.

Like all things on the spectrum of spectacular and tragic, it is the Black women who are the blueprint. Unfortunately for our children, it is the negative perception of the oversexualized Black girl that sets the standard of sexual violence done to children of color.

These rotted roots go back to the era of Black enslavement, when white enslavers justified raping young Black girls by stating that it was in their nature to be sexually active. Their justifications went beyond the "They asked for it" rhetoric and nestled deeply into the absurdity of "This is what they were made for." The enslaver's imagination decided that his victim's sole purpose was to be raped—raped to produce more slaves and raped to please the sexual appetite of white maleness. The younger the Black girl, the better, because she'd be able to produce more children throughout her lifetime. Black girls and Black women were only viewed as capital and labor. The more children one would have, the more capital she would gain. The more rapes she experienced, the greater the contribution she would make to the American economy. Thus, the Black girl—sweet, innocent, and deserving of tenderhearted care—was unable to control the ways in which her darling melanin-rich body was oversexualized. She became the sexual object used to create American wealth and to please the truly demonic desires of the enslaver.

When I behold the story of Salome, I also hold the violence done to all the young enslaved Black girls unjustly associated with the "Jezebel archetype." This archetype was born from a misinterpretation of the story of Queen Jezebel, a ruthless leader whose sin was idolatry, not sex. Black girls and women became villainized under this misinterpretation, and their hypersexualized bodies were made objects of blame for the "pure and pious white men" who were tempted by their sexuality. Though the biblical Jezebel's sin was idolatry and not sexuality, when Black women are called Jezebels (a racial slur against Black women), it is confirmation that their bodies are idolatrous tools tempting white men from their positions of piety. Black girls, like Salome, are all children used as props to uphold a story of greatness. For Salome, it's her objectified body that upholds the Christian narrative of John the Baptist's tragic death, propelling him into the constellation of legendary figures within Christendom. For enslaved Black girls, it is their objectified and violated bodies that moved the American economy forward, propelling the mythos of the great American dream. America's dream, often told in tandem with the prosperity gospel's religious zeal, is the nightmare of thousands of enslaved Black girls forced to become mothers whose children were forcibly removed from their arms just so the cycle would be repeated.

It is rare for me to meet a person who has wept for Salome. In the same vein, I rarely meet people weeping for the Black girls who have been sexually abused, raped, and turned into the villains within their nightmare existence entitled the American dream. But I'm not one of those people who leave these realities in the past. The violence of yesterday creates the mythos of today. Healing wounds and ending harms require us to confront the ways we've been taught to believe lies that still endanger Black girls. The fact is that the myth of the young Jezebel still exists today. It forms the policies of our schools, the bylaws of our sanctuaries, the structure of our failed carceral systems, the interventions done by social service organizations, and our disillusioned perceptions of a child's sexuality. "At nearly 19 percent, the rate of sexual victimization for Black girls and young women is amongst the highest for any group in the nation," writes Monique W. Morris in her book *Pushout: The Criminalization of Black Girls in Schools.* "Girls experience sexual assault, objectification, or being seen as hypersexual in many places. . . . It's a web that not only entangles Black girls' bodies but can also ensnare their minds."[5]

The moral code of enslavement made the victim-blaming of Black-girl sexual violence survivors a cultural norm. Black girls are blamed for their seductive bodies and punished with rape as a form of domesticating their hypersexualized forms. Hypersexualization of a child's body is done by a society that has socialized the bodies of white women as its cultural ideal. Black girls are punished for existing. The narrative surrounding their punishment was that it was for a greater good. The oppressor's imagination implanted the cultural belief that a Black girl was so seductive that she had the power to exploit a man's weakness and make him fall into the sinful act of betraying his race. Never mind that rape, child violence, labor exploitation, abduction, and enslavement are sins listed in the Bible. The enslaver believed himself God and made Black women his foe, creating a carceral logic that would punish Black women throughout the generations.

A 2017 survey conducted by Jamilia J. Blake of Texas A&M University revealed that adults who work in public service jobs (education, law enforcement, youth development, etc.) believe Black girls between the ages of five and fourteen years old to be less innocent and more adultlike than white girls of the same age.[6] This type of socialization compresses the ages of children and places harsher standards on them than their peers whose identities exist elsewhere along the spectrum of gender and race. Adultification turns children into criminals. Harsher punishments await Black girls who are trying to exist. Assuming Black girls have adultlike characteristics means their behavior and motivations are narrated by the imaginations of people who have and will violate their bodies. There are few safe spaces for Black girls. They navigate through a world socialized to blame them for the atrocities done to their bodies, and they are blamed for having poor behavior or conduct. Dress codes and uniforms in schools become weapons to criticize the Black female body and compare it to the "goodness" of a white child's physical development. Purity culture within our churches *automatically* villainizes Black girls' bodies because, no matter what they wear or what they do, whiteness has already deemed their presence as too sexual. Statements like "You should have known better," or "You're being disrespectful," or "Don't act too grown," and the asking of invasive questions regarding sexual activity are commonly heard by Black girls regardless of the public institution they're in. It's a multitiered system of mental warfare done to the minds of children: navigating safety in unsafe terrain, then being punished for having poor behavior while navigating that unsafe terrain, then being blamed when violence happens and having little to no support because of the ways our society has socialized us to blame Black girls.

Innocence is not simply a characteristic or a quality that is attributed by an adult to a child. Innocence is not a privilege offered to some. Innocence is not a standard children must strive for. Innocence is a *developmental necessity* and a lens that Black girls deserve. The biblical story of Salome presents her as a murderous temptress undeserving of our grace, and our society does the same with Black girls. To recognize children as innocent would compel us to operate in a way that allows them to flourish. We have to resocialize ourselves and our society to recognize that the ways it views Black girls is a direct result of the enslaver's imagination. Uproot their false narratives and decenter their morality structure from our own. The entire construct of whiteness is a system of grooming, made to turn Black girls into sexualized objects who are trafficked into carceral systems that will continue to harm them. If we dedicate ourselves to protecting Black girls—and all children of color—from the multilayered violence they face, we must recognize that they, like Salome, are victims and survivors of generational harm and adverse childhood experiences.

From 1995 to 1997, medical researchers Vincent J. Felitti and Robert Anda conducted a survey of 17,421 people and made what is arguably the greatest public health finding of our time.

In the 1980s, Felitti was the chief of Kaiser Permanente's Department of Preventative Medicine in San Diego. Many of his patients were white, middle-class people classified as obese. Felitti was trying to discover why more than half of his patients in the obesity clinic dropped out of the program while they were showing positive results (weight loss) and then gained weight rapidly upon leaving. He decided to have face-to-face interviews with them. Nearly every interviewee told him about suffering from childhood sexual abuse. His team, which conducted interviews with about one hundred additional people, had the same findings. Felitti discovered that he was treating the coping mechanism (i.e., eating addiction) as the illness instead of the symptom.

At the same time, Anda was a medical epidemiologist at the Centers for Disease Control who was studying depression and its impact on people with coronary heart disease. His findings showed that depression and feelings of hopelessness weren't random. While Felitti was interested in the correlation between child sexual abuse and addiction, Anda was interested in discovering if there was a predictor for feelings of hopelessness.

Together with their team of researchers, Felitti and Anda did a megastudy of 17,421 people in San Diego to discover if childhood trauma impacted adult health. Their findings became known as the study of Adverse Childhood Experiences, or ACEs. The ACEs study disproved two mindsets: (1) that risk factors for disease and early death are random, and (2) that people can get over the harm they experienced in childhood without negative side effects. In doing so, the ACEs study discovered that there is a powerful relationship between childhood harm and our physical, emotional, and mental health as adults.

In 2008, Nadine Burke Harris, a Black Canadian-American pediatrician who eventually became California's first surgeon general, read the ACEs study and gained language to explain the connection between childhood traumatic experiences and health problems. Two years later she cofounded the Adverse Childhood Experiences project, which created a clinical model for recognizing ACEs and treating toxic stress in children by undoing the biological and neurodevelopmental harm that arose from experiencing different forms of violence, neglect, and abuse. The flagship project was in the Bayview–Hunters Point neighborhood in San Francisco, which was very ethnically diverse in contrast to the original ACEs study out of San Diego. At the time, this neighborhood boasted the highest Black population in San Francisco. The Adverse Childhood Experiences project pioneered ways to integrate different forms of care—health care; mental health care; and research, policy, community, and family support—to help children heal and build resilience.

I'm a fan of the work done by the doctors, researchers, and practitioners who paved this path for providing care-centered models for children experiencing harm. But there's a caveat. With all the amazing research, findings, and educational programming that exists to reverse the effects of ACEs and lower the amount of ACEs for future generations, I've noticed how the topic of racial violence is a suggestive footnote. I've gone to a lot of conferences on childhood trauma and find that a small fraction of the education—which is consistently given by a white person—includes race as an honorable mention but not a core issue. Racial violence becomes an endcap mentioned with a seemingly dismissive tone. There seems to be a great divide on whose childhood trauma is studied, whose healing modalities are pioneered, and who gets to educate the masses on it.

In 2022, I attended a four-day conference on creating trauma-informed environments for children. The lead educator was a white woman who was very thorough with her information but, true to form, left the topic of racialized violence to one sentence out of the entire sixteen-hour teaching series. During Q&A time, a participant asked the educator what to do about a member of her local school board who was openly racist, proudly boasted of how he attended the storming of the Capitol on January 6, 2021, and was building a case for "culture wars" within the district. The educator, who had been very thorough in providing all the scientific information on how trauma negatively impacts a child's well-being, paused and said, "I prefer to lead with empathy." And that was her complete answer.

My problem with the whole situation was that she wanted the participant—who was clearly concerned for her children and their classmates—to be empathetic toward a grown man who pays taxes and makes his own decisions, a racist man who encourages doing harm to

Black and non-Black children of color. While I believe in empathy, I don't believe in extending the benefit of the doubt to someone who harms children. The children—specifically the children of color who attended school board meetings and were vocal about experiencing racism on their campuses—were left out of the conversation, their feelings and development nullified in comparison to the adults'.

This too is how adultification operates. It assumes that children of color need less nurturing, protection, support, and comfort. To adultify children is not only to disregard the harm they're experiencing but also to assume they can handle the hurt. In doing so, the attention and care go to the person of privilege. It was disappointing to experience this form of violence at a conference on trauma-informed care practices for children.

Children of color are expected to navigate the world as adults. It doesn't matter how trauma-informed someone is; when their allegiance is to the standards set by narratives of white supremacy, then they too will cause harm to children of color. My experience at that trauma-informed-care workshop was just one out of a multitude of negative experiences I've had in this field. I am left to wonder if the movement for trauma-informed care is slowly molding itself into a form of supremacy that chooses which children deserve care. "Trauma-informed" does not always mean "privilege-aware" or "system-dismantling," and that's a travesty.

I was five or six the first time my developing body was objectified. At eight years old, my body began developing curves. When I was ten, a grown man began making lewd remarks to me during a family party. I can barely remember this interaction but will never forget the way he licked his lips, slid closer to me on the couch, and told me that I was *so sexy*. By twelve, I had classmates commenting on my body and asking about my hips. At fourteen a peer came up to me and told me that I needed to cover up my body. I was fifteen when a teacher publicly accused me of being a disruptive flirt. The simple act of smiling at people began to stir anxiety. By sixteen, grown men would follow me, ask my age, and try to flirt a different answer out of me. At seventeen I joined an evangelical church and believed the theologies of purity would save me from a lifetime of undeserved sexual violence.

Every time I recount these memories of my Black girlhood inter-rupted by society's obsession with villainizing the Black female body, I recall all the ways my humanity was removed. A stereotype was made more important than my soul. I often wonder how many Black girls become Black women who have had their humanity flattened, falsely accused, bruised, and violated in this society whose foundation was built on their continual demoralization.

As a mother, I've learned it is more important to center safety over theology when choosing which faith community to raise my children in. Theology can be altered, manipulated, and faked. You can't do the same with safety because, unlike theology, safety does not exist on a spectrum. It doesn't matter how blessed, holy, or upright a church may claim itself to be. It doesn't matter if the congregants call them-selves family and host frequent events. If the children aren't safe, leave the community alone. God has no footing there.

I learned this lesson when I was a new mother filled with exhaus-tion and anxious wonderings of whether or not I was "doing this right." At that time, I participated heavily in the evangelical church we attended. We went to multiple events, attended service regularly, and were frequent participants in small group gatherings. At one church gathering, I was holding my daughter, a sweet little four-month-old cooing bundle of joy. She and I were enjoying the sweet-ness of this moment, and I thought I was doing right by her and God by attending that church gathering. The moment cracked when an elderly white man who had a sparkling reputation among the con-gregants looked at my daughter and sweetly said, "She's so exotic."

At a mere four months old, my daughter was othered and posi-tioned to become a sexual object for the white gaze. In that moment I became keenly aware of what harm awaited my darling baby girl if I chose to stay and allow whiteness and maleness to absorb my sweet girl's soul by assigning it to the narratives that have harmed young girls for centuries.

Our children deserve better.

Chapter Eleven

The Woman Caught in Adultery

The scribes and the Pharisees brought a woman who had been caught in adultery, and, making her stand before all of them, they said to him, "Teacher, this woman was caught in the very act of committing adultery. Now in the law Moses commanded us to stone such women. Now what do you say?" They said this to test him, so that they might have some charge to bring against him. Jesus bent down and wrote with his finger on the ground. When they kept on questioning him, he straightened up and said to them, "Let anyone among you who is without sin be the first to throw a stone at her." And once again he bent down and wrote on the ground. When they heard it, they went away, one by one, beginning with the elders, and Jesus was left alone with the woman standing before him. Jesus straightened up and said to her, "Woman, where are they? Has no one condemned you?" She said, "No one, sir." And Jesus said, "Neither do I condemn you. Go your way, and from now on do not sin again."

—John 8:3–11

Tumah

Clitoris comes from the
Greek word kleitoris.

It's a noun meaning hill.
It's a verb meaning rub.

I was an adult when an elder
recommended I hold a mirror

to myself and introduce pleasure
into the faultline.

              "You can't trust
yourself if you don't know yourself.

How do you expect to care for others
If you can't extend care to yourself?"

self sex is described as ghost
sex. Gentle caresses are more

foreign than the wounds we share.

If you let your touch heal you. You
will gain a faith that moves mountains

Pleasure Activism

I look down at my phone to find the time. It's 1 a.m.. I'm exhausted. I'll probably be shaking feather pieces out of my hair for the next few days and the glitter—oh God, the glitter—will more than likely show up in the shower. Luckily, there are no rips in my fishnets, and my heels are comfy as ever. I'll count that as a good thing. I carefully take off the costume bra and wipe the sweat off my face. My makeup rubs off a little as well. Thank God for Kia; he's a wonder at righting all the wrongs I put with my makeup. The other performers are telling stories and laughing about the night as another one gets ready for her go-go set. Others are marking their dance steps: step, step, bend, turn, and pose—pop that booty, hold your core, aaaaand smile. Here we were, a bunch of dancers in this burlesque company, going through another night of performing fantasy and conjuring arousal. But really we were a community of folks who enjoyed each other's company, laughed heartily, and talked openly with each other about the things we were enduring in our day jobs, love lives, and everything in between.

I started dancing burlesque after graduating college in 2010. I danced extensively in college and wanted to be a part of a company; this opportunity fell in my lap. There are different types of burlesque dance; ours was neoburlesque that was heavily inspired by the choreography and aesthetic of the Pussy Cat Dolls: hip-hop and jazz choreography in heels and lingerie with makeup and face jewels on artistically lit stages. I loved many things about it: the choreography, the community, the ways we laughed heartily. Stripping happens in burlesque, but the art form is more than what is deemed vulgar. Burlesque is the practice of creating anticipation while maintaining control, and for those of us who were formed in multiple environments of harm, it becomes an art form that allows us to expand our capacity for control. Flirting had its purpose, costumes were craftily made, whole conversations happened in a smile, and every gesture—big or small—was an intentional redirection. I loved it. What I didn't love was the overwhelming shame that eventually led me to quit burlesque. The shame wasn't my own; it was given to me by the purity culture scripts that constantly ran through my head and from family members who were disappointed that I "wasted" my college degree only to "become a stripper." My career as a burlesque dancer was much like watching the sunset: it was vibrant and beautiful, but it slowly faded until all that was left was the ambiguity of night. I quit the art form about two years later. I was sitting in front of the church that eventually became a place of deep trauma and had my last phone call with the director and choreographer. I told him I couldn't do it anymore, hung up the phone, and recommitted my life to being pure.

I wish I hadn't done that.

Let me rephrase that: I wish I could go back into that moment to hold the hand of my younger self and tell her that this decision she's making is based off a false belief that her pleasure is to be found in what other people tell her is God's approval. I wish I had held the face of my younger self and said, "Let's learn how to trust ourselves enough to see that our body is good instead of running toward an institution that shames us into objectified submission." I sincerely wish I could have told myself that any place that indoctrinates me to believe in a binary—the church versus the world, my body versus my spirit, my pleasure versus my salvation—is the true harbinger of wrongdoing. But I can't go back in time. The best gift I can give to my younger self is to deconstruct my own understanding of purity. I'd have to start with the law of Moses and find God there.

Jesus was a pleasure activist. To be a pleasure activist is to advocate for the pleasure of all and to also pursue advocacy work with pleasure as a liberating practice. As adrienne maree brown writes, "Pleasure activism is about learning what it means to be satisfiable, to generate, from within and from between us, an abundance from which we can all have enough."[1] Once I started reading the Gospels from the perspective of pleasure activism, I began to understand Jesus in a way that heals me. I've spent much of my adult life in the Christian paradox of accessing God's abundant love and infinite power through strict self-restraint and shame. Expanding my spirituality beyond that paradox requires me to read the life of Jesus in ways that reject policing and carceral logics.

There was intentionality to the time frame in which Jesus left the heavenly realm and entered our world. Jesus was born in the land of Palestine, which was violently occupied by the colonizing Roman Empire. He barely survived infanticide and became a child refugee seeking asylum in Egypt. He eventually returned home to Galilee and grew up in multiple layers of oppression. His hometown was known for its fertile soil and profitable harvests. His community's farm labor and natural resources were exploited so that the Roman Empire could thrive. Jesus lived under Moses' laws and knew them as intimately as he knew himself, but he also knew that the fallacy of human laws is found in the human beings who enforce them with ulterior motives. Moses' laws were given to the Israelites after generations of unfathomable oppression and enslavement in Egypt. The laws were built for liberation, healing, and community care.

I admit that I have a tough time with analyzing the laws of Moses because my Christian upbringing centered supersessionist theologies that erase Jews from their holy texts. I remember statements such as "The laws don't apply to us," "We are set free in Christ," and "That's *the old* covenant; this is *the new* covenant." But those statements cause harm and bolster antisemitic violence. It wasn't until I started reading the writings of feminist rabbis that I was able to build a nonproblematic relationship with God's laws. An eye-opening lesson was on the concept of purity in the laws. The words in these texts are *tumah* (impure) and *tahor* (pure). My previous readings of Scripture taught me to pursue *tahor* and despise the things (like seeing a dead body, being on my period, ejaculation) that bring *tumah* into my life. But that's wrong! *Tahor* and *tumah* aren't in a battle of good versus evil. Instead, they offer an invitation into a mode of contemplation. As Rabbi Rachel Adler explains, "*Tumah* is the result of our confrontation with the fact of our own mortality. It is the going down into darkness. . . . *Tumah* is devil or frightening only when there is no further life. Otherwise, *tumah* is simply part of the human cycle. To be *tameh* [i.e., to be in a state of *tumah*] is not wrong or bad. Often it is necessary and sometimes it is mandatory."[2]

I choose to believe that the law of Moses gifts us with the holiness of knowing our humanity and contemplating how finite it is. This includes honoring the dead, having sex, giving birth, and allowing my period to set a boundary for how much energy I'm going to exert that day. (When the cervix starts cramping and the blood starts flow-ing, I am committed to giving 60 percent of my energy to and eating half my weight in dark chocolate.) These embodied forms of contem-plation help us enjoy life and connect deeply with others, and they prepare us for a deeper connection with God when we are *tahor*.[3]

With that reading in mind, it would be remiss of me to say that the Pharisees are the bad guys. I think that kind of theology is antisemitic. The Pharisees were doing what they could to protect their commu-nity—their brethren—from the daily threat of harm that came from living in an occupied land. I think the Pharisees, like many Christians today, sought to do right by the law so that they would be protected by God. This does not mean they're evil; it means they're people who are intimately acquainted with the pressure that comes with leadership under an oppressive reign. They deserve our compassion as well as our critique. When reading the Gospels through these lenses, I find that the purveyor of violence is not Judaism but the Romans, who occupied their homeland with militaristic might and supremacist ideologies. People living under violent systems can unknowingly reconstruct the same violence within their own communities. That violence is made apparent when the Pharisees use the adulteress to confront Jesus.

There have been a lot of words to describe this woman, but never a name. The Christian spaces I grew up in lumped her in with the prostitutes of the Bible. I once believed those teachings, but there's no scholarship indicating that she was a sex worker. *Adulteress* can mean many things: one who has sex before marriage, one who is cheating on her spouse, or even one who has been assaulted or raped, in some cases. We don't know her; we only know the shame placed upon her. In the face of her public shame and the looming threat of being stoned to death, Jesus thwarts the Pharisees by saying, "Let anyone among you who is without sin be the first to throw a stone at her" (John 8:7). I think there's a deeper layer here that we people living under the violence of a supremacist empire must ask ourselves as we create communities of resistance and liberation: "When have your perfectionism and respectability truly saved you? Will shaming someone else's *tumah*—their embodied contemplation of humanity—in our time of survival be a useful tool in an empire such as this? How will shame deepen our connection with one another and with God?"

The reason why I believe Jesus was a pleasure activist was because he, too, centered safety within his organizing and liberating work. He was infamous for spending time with sex workers and "sinners." My Bible teachers and mentors taught me that Jesus spent time with them to convert them through his care. I don't know if that answer works for me anymore. I think Jesus spent time with them because they lived in a violent and traumatic era of their people's history and he wanted them to be safe as they did what they could to experience pleasure while living under constant threat. He wanted to empower them to be a community that harnesses the erotic energy of pleasure to care for and nourish one another. This doesn't mean that the Christ was a hedonist, taking part in orgies or drunken antics. Rather, Jesus sought to do his community organizing and liberating work among people who were honest about the harm they experienced and wanted to protect each other instead of perfecting each other. Not once do the Gospels mention a follower of Jesus experiencing an overdose, getting kidnapped, abusing children, or getting murdered by a john. That speaks volumes.

I am in the process of building a love ethic that rebukes shame, reduces harm, and celebrates our embodiment. Healing from many forms of violence, including spiritual abuse, led me to unapologetically center my capacity for control, care, and consent. I believe those three pillars are necessary parts of healing, but we can approach those three pillars in different ways. I gained my three pillars through talk therapy, journaling, and somatic healing. Whitney, my trans-femme friend, has the same three pillars in her personal love ethic and as a community organizer. She gained hers through engaging in trauma-informed kink workshops that allowed her to access pleasure as a tool to build her capacity for consent. I found it fascinating that these elements of pleasure villainized by conservative and abusive Christian environments were the same elements that healed people and created communities of care and liberation. Moreover, I became invested in the ways that consent can be given back to those who have been objectified and violated.

I decided that in order to share this information I would need to learn from those who are facilitating these healing workshops within our communities. I met with Coach Felyne, a Black queer mother of two and body enthusiast who created the Center for Body Autonomy to learn about the ways reclaiming our pleasure restores our capacity for consent and care. Coach Felyne is the creator of Trauma-Informed Consensual Kink (TICK), a program introducing people to how consent shows up in the kink world and the creation of consent protocols to expand our experience of kink in a way that prevents unwanted harm. In her words:

> We created TICK with the assumption that we move into a pleasure situation understanding that this person we're engaging with has experienced trauma, [and that] we have also experienced trauma. And so those pieces have to be connected, right? Our idea within TICK is that we are always, (1) considering that we all experience trauma, (2) that there is a way for us to possibly navigate it, and (3) that when harm is caused we can activate some of the knowledge that we have within our own bodies. It includes the possibility that harm could be caused. And that's dependent upon what happens, and it's also dependent upon who's involved. And through that, we take into consideration some of those things that have lasting influence: what accountability looks like for people of color in carceral systems.
>
> We live in a world where we can unknowingly re-create the same harm [we experienced] We don't want to re-create those same systems. Instead, we ask what it requires of us to move into restoration, to acknowledge harm, even unintentional harm, or intentional harm, and being able to have some sort of framework that we can dive into that says our work doesn't have to re-create this system. And our work is also always imagining how have we done it and how do we want to do it in the future.[4]

Listening to Coach Felyne made me consider the power of *tumah* in rewriting how we define ourselves outside of the harm we've experienced in abusive environments built on carceral logic. Sex can be a pathway to reducing harm, building connection, and facilitating healing for people who have been objectified and dehumanized and who are descendants of colonization and genocide.

I named kink as a pathway toward healing, but let me clarify that kink is not strictly about sex. Kink is the experience of being expansive. As Coach Felyne explained:

> As Black people, we're exposed to numerous types of trauma throughout the day, whether that be going to work, going into the library, going into a bank to try to get a loan, going to get the car repaired, understanding what our children are going through at any given moment, and being able to relate to that. And so there's so much trauma that happens that is absolutely without our consent. But kink gives us exploration within Blackness. [Let's say] I'm a nurturer, and let's say that in my nurturing I desire to cook delicious meals and feed them to someone who is going to enjoy a delicious meal. To do so doesn't mean that I am a submissive creating meals for the person who wants to eat. It means that I'm providing an energy that they will be able to [see me in] that dynamic. And so kink opens us up to the expansiveness of living outside of a culturally made box for us. And I love that it is interconnected. As we explore our kink, as we discover the multitudes of who we are, it's not separate from how we live our lives. It is a part of the continuum of who we are, and the ancestral knowledge of pleasure being created for pleasure.[5]

Pleasure lives in the body. Pleasure requires us to be present with ourselves and to ask, "Is this OK?" or "Am I comfortable?"—and my favorite question: "Do I want this right now?"

We can't talk about pleasure without talking about sex and all the justifications used to keep sex out of the conversation or to villainize sexual activity. Sex is a part of pleasure, but it's not the whole of it. Pleasure is the act of being deeply present in our aliveness through doing what feels good within the context of personal and interrelational safety. To experience pleasure is to tap into an erotic energy that nourishes and empowers us to create necessary pathways on this good road toward liberation.

Pleasure allows us to step into the fullness of ourselves, as it invites us into being set free from the violent stereotypes and archetypes that were created by the oppressive systems that dehumanize us. Contemplating this reminds me of the common Christian sayings like, "I am set free," "I am born again," and "You are made new." What if the art of being made new is not found in restrictive, shame-filled, and predatory religious practices? What if it's done through the work of restoring ourselves to the experience of pleasure? And, most importantly, what happens if we stop living in the "what if" and transform these curiosities into our reality?

When the Pharisees confront Jesus with the woman caught in adultery, their intention is to confound and trap him by shaming her. But Jesus isn't swayed. He does not use her life as an example of what is or isn't righteous. When the Pharisees leave, Jesus stands with her to determine whether she was condemned. She wasn't. "Neither do I condemn you," says Jesus. "Go your way, and from now on do not sin again" (8:11).

We don't know what sort of situation the woman was caught in. Jesus shows no interest in finding out what it is. The only detail Jesus cares about is whether she understands that she isn't condemned. Then he tells her to leave and not to sin again. I used to believe the "sin" Jesus refers to is adultery, but now I realize her true sin was letting a violent empire control her and her community.

My heart flutters at the thought of Jesus saying, "Neither do I condemn you." These are words that I need to hear on my own healing journey. They are a gift I want to give to those who are on their own journey toward liberation.

> Are you learning how to advocate for yourself and others? *I don't condemn you.*
> Are you rejecting your allegiance to power? *I don't condemn you.*
> Are you dismantling white imperialist cisgender patriarchy? *I don't condemn you.*
> Are you disentangling yourself from purity culture? *I don't condemn you.*
> Are you decolonizing and de-imperializing? *I don't condemn you.*

Are you letting your rage bless your liberation? *I don't condemn you.*

Are you ending the conspiracy of silence and joining a community of truth tellers? *I don't condemn you.*

Are you ending the sexual invisibilization of queer, trans, and disabled people? *I don't condemn you.*

Are you healing your insecure attachments? *I don't condemn you.*

Are you protecting children of color from adultification? *I don't condemn you.*

Are you dignifying your humanity by reclaiming your pleasure? *I don't condemn you.*

I'm still on this journey of blending pleasure activism with spiritual growth. I'm finding holiness in discovering our unknown kinks and creating systems of safety that reshape our identities away from white imperialist cisgender patriarchal–created archetypes forced on us and our ancestors. The hardest work I've done (and will continue to do) is untether myself from believing the center of morality is found in the people who have caused and continue to perpetuate atrocities.

I will always be a whore to them—deviant, sexual, and prioritizing my safety and pleasure over their flaccid god complex. To be labeled a whore in an empire and a religion system that has done everything they can to control my body means that I've unshackled myself from their oppressive expectations. My life is my own. It's not an instrument used to perpetuate generational harms done to me, my community, and my ancestors. I join the long line of pleasure activists, community builders, birthworkers, and survivors building communities of safety in the rubble of every apocalypse white imperialist cisgender patriarchy created.

Call me a whore, but never forget I'm the hero too.

Epilogue

An Open Letter to Survivors

Darling,

I believe you.

As the pain crashes and the memories crest, as your heart shatters and you scream into the thickened silence, as you crave to be known and held, I believe you. I believe what happened to you. It was awful and unspeakable. I do not know what happened in your life, and I won't press you to share the horrors if you are not ready to. It doesn't matter what I know or what I don't know; it matters that I believe you. And I do. I believe every tear, scream, roar, and silence. I weep alongside you for what has been stolen and beg for there to be moments of ease as we pursue what will be restored. You are not a liar or an attention-seeker or whatever awful thing someone else has accused you of. You are precious. You are worthy of safety and secure relationships.

I believe you, and I believe *in* you. Because of this I must say a necessary truth: it's not your fault. I wish I could say this to you again and again until it becomes the truth echoing through your inner being. It's not your fault. It's not your fault. It's not your fault. My darling, your skeleton is heavy with the weight of other peoples' sins. Their greed, ignorance, violence, and insecurity were never meant to be your burden. And yet they are. We can't deny it. It would be foolish of me to say that you can simply uncloak yourself from someone else's action. We've been blamed for the monstrosity. We carry the blame like palimpsest on our skin for all to see, all while wishing impossible wishes like *If only they could see me and understand.* I know what it means to crave understanding and to sit alone asking myself if I deserved it. I remember how people would ask, "Why are you like this?" or "Why can't you get over it?" There are days when I catch myself praying for unending sleep or feeling like a sustained fire that will burn everything down to make the memories disappear. I know how our hurt can hurt others, how we can create pain in places where we need understanding. The past will haunt our present, turning us into tactile ghosts. We don't deserve the unspeakable things that have bored twisted holes in our souls. Yet here we are trying the best we can to clean up the mess made by people, the empires they worship, and the awful ways they decide to cope with their hurts. I don't know what happened to you, but I know this: your body was not created to hold another person's downfall. Your body was created for love, and I pray we can return you to it.

These truths are the only words I can give to connect my heart to yours. I believe you. It's not your fault. I hope you learn to string these truths like beads and wear it around your neck every day. Decorate yourself with it, let it be the pendant that shines forth from your heart. Let it dangle there and be the ever-present reminder that you deserve more than this world has given.

With all my love and understanding,
Camille

Acknowledgments

This book exists because of the people who have loved me throughout the years.

Thank you to my loving husband, who held me during the many moments when I wept over our exit from evangelicalism. Thank you for reminding me that we are bigger than the claustrophobic corners they put us in. You are my best friend, *mi cariño,* and my most earnest supporter.

Many thanks to my children for all the love they pour in and all the lessons they pour out. Thank you for the ways you've inspired me to tell the truth, shame the devil, and create a better world for you.

I must thank my therapist, Jasmine Walker, for all the ways she has nurtured me with empathy, wisdom, and care. Thank you for being a constant source of compassion and insight within my life and throughout my healing process. I wholeheartedly appreciate you.

Thank you to the family members who carried me when I did not even know myself: my brother, elders, and our many cousins—the Allens, Bilogs, Extras, Mendozas, Enriquezes, Strongs, and Panganibans. I thank my mother for the love that she has given me, the ways she protected me, and the depth of care that she continues to greet me with. I am a mama's girl through and through. And to my father, I love you with a complicated love, and my heart remains connected to yours. I wish the world had been better to you so that you might have been better to me. But I know you loved in the only way you knew how and, though it hurt, I am grateful you stayed.

My deep and unending gratitude goes to my chosen family—Alicia Crosby Mack, Robert Monson, and Christine Yi Suh—who cared for, supported, and challenged me throughout the process of writing this book. Your love is found in the tenderness of each word. Thank you, Alicia, for being the first person with whom I shared the idea of this book. Thank you for reminding me that the stories in Scripture are raggedy and that it's OK to love these stories enough to tell the truth about them.

A big ol' shout out and warm embrace goes to the two churches—the Church We Hope For in Monrovia, California, and One Life City Church in Fullerton, California—who were gentle and gracious to me and my family during the writing of this book. I could not put finger to keyboard during the hardest times had it not been for your check-ins, babysitting, meal trains, and sending us emergency craft supplies when all my kids were sick with multiple illnesses and I had to finish a chapter during quarantine. My loving thanks goes especially to Bobby Harrison and Ines Velasquez-McBryde. You gifted me with a hope that helped me write about hope.

During the year I wrote this book, I had the great pleasure of participating in a writing retreat with the organization Roots.Wounds. Words. It changed my life. Had it not been for the organizing work of Nicole Shawan Junior and Willow, this book would be different. Thank you to my poetry cohort—Xan Phillips, Czaerra Ucol, Erin Jin Mei O'Malley, Gabriel Hendrix, Gray Agpalo, Haru Matsuura, Makshya Tolbert, Monica, Nikita Lavrews, RaeJeana Brooks, Solange Azor, and Travis Love—for inspiring me to add poetry, reject form, take up space, and exploit the English language in order to find new pathways to hope. I am grateful for each of you and wholeheartedly believe in the power of your presence and words.

This book exists because Ashley Sunghae reached out to me and said, "I think you have a book in you." Before that moment I only called myself a writer in the silent spaces of my head. Thank you for seeing me. Thank you for reaching out. Thank you for listening to the God that guides us and believing that I could do something beyond the world's expectations of me. A special and deeply heartfelt thanks goes to my agent, Trinity McFadden, and the team at The Bindery Agency. Thank you for existing, and thank you for taking a chance on me. Trinity, your encouragement and enthusiasm have been a gift throughout this entire process. I am very grateful for you. My love goes to Dr. Chanequa Walker-Barnes, who said yes to writing this book's foreword. I have admired you for so long and just about cried when you agreed to contribute. I am glad to now call you friend. And thank you to my editor, Jessica Miller Kelley, who has kept each word accountable to our faith and to our communities. I cherish you.

There's nothing holier than a group chat. I must thank the incredible women who kept me sane and let me cry and laugh and laugh and cry during this whole writing process. First, let me thank my darling Heather Barrett for keeping up with me via Marco Polo. Our friendship throughout these years is a gift. I'm so grateful to have you as my friend and sister to cheer me on and to stress out with you as we raise our kids together and miles apart. Thanks to the women of the #FFF crew: Meleca Consultado, Alicia McCormick, Nallely López, Claudia Y. Salazar, Noelle Delacruz, Ralonda Dittmar, and Ruthi Hoffman Hanchett. Your memes got me through the loneliness of writing. I am blessed to be known, seen, and celebrated by you. To my crew of leos—Heidi Elizabeth Lepe, Meleca Consultado, Alma Carrillo, Esperanza Gene, and Sandy Saravia—our high-energy conversations and deep connections have been a highlight throughout the second half of writing this book. Thank you for reminding me of what sisterhood looks like. A special thanks to my reading buddy Denise Peñacerrada Kruse. It is an honor to journey with you to read the hidden stories of our kababayan and gossip as our ancestors did. To my friends in the "Holy Haters," "Writers Against Content Creation," "Black Girl Softness," and "Cute and Chronically Ill" group chats, I *needed* you during those times when I had to consciously say no to things that distracted me from my art. You are my family.

I am so grateful for the community of Black women who lifted me up and crowdsourced mutual aid during the time when my family struggled. To Rose J. Percy, Sharifa Stevens, and Alicia Crosby: thank you for your love and your tender care. I made it to the finish line with your love to carry me. And thank you for bringing in the folks who helped me get to the finish line. I am so grateful for my finish-line team who gave me and my family tangible care through mutual aid. You are all indelible pieces to this story, and I pray your names are written in the book of life, and (just in case) I want to include your names in this book because it wouldn't exist without your donations to the community care fund: Eugene Kim, Kaitlin Curtice, Annette Adams, Timothy Yoong Jie Gen, Micah "JMarie" Morgan, Jenai Auman, Geneva Moore, Cristina Hernandez, Israel Cawley, Jill Jensen, Sarah Bessey, Donna Burkland, Debra Tripp, Heather Barrett, Brenda Luu, Jeanne Porter King, Jaylin Chacon, Meleca Consultado, Elaine Belze, Mye Love, Robert McBryde, Robert Monson, Kathleen Lunson, Marielle Thomas, and Sharifa Stevens. Thank you. Bless you. You are a light in my life and evidence that a better world is possible.

I must thank the ancestors and the God who made us. I do not know what happens beyond the passing, but I know without a doubt that you walk this earth with me and through me. I am never alone, for God is with me, and my ancestors brought their great cloud of witnesses to sustain my steps.

Finally, I thank you, dear reader, for choosing this book. I pray these words are a balm.

Notes

Foreword

1. Marjorie Partch, "Katie Cannon," in *Contemporary Black Biography*, vol. 10, ed. L. Mpho Mabunda (Detroit: Gale, 1996), 26.

Prologue

1. Iris Marion Young, "Five Faces of Oppression," in *Oppression, Privilege, & Resistance*, ed. Lisa Heldke and Peg O'Connor (New York: McGraw Hill, 2004), 37–63.
2. Young, "Five Faces of Oppression," 52–53.
3. UN Women, "Frequently Asked Questions: Types of Violence against Women and Girls," https://www.unwomen.org/en/what-we-do/ending-violence-against-women/faqs/types-of-violence.
4. Cristena Cleveland, *God Is a Black Woman* (New York: HarperCollins, 2022), 58.
5. Maharaj "Raju" Desai, "Critical Kapwa: Possibilities of Collective Healing from Colonial Trauma," *Educational Perspectives* 48, nos. 1 and 2 (2016): 34–40.
6. Sarah Lamble, "Practicing Everyday Abolition," Abolitionist Futures, August 2019, https://abolitionistfutures.com/latest-news/practising-everyday-abolition.

Chapter 1: Eve

1. H. G. Reza, "Navy to Stop Recruiting Filipino Nationals: Defense: The End of the Military Base Agreement with the Philippines Will Terminate the Nearly Century-Old Program," *Los Angeles Times*, February 27, 1992, https://www.latimes.com/archives/la-xpm-1992-02-27-me-3911-story.html.
2. International Labour Organization, "Labour Migration in the Philippines," https://www.ilo.org/manila/areasofwork/labour-migration/lang--en/index.htm.
3. Eugene F. Roger, *Blood Theology: Seeing Red in Body and God-Talk* (Cambridge: Cambridge University Press, 2021), 85.

4. Mohamed A. Zeidan, Sarah Igoe, Clas Linnman, Vitalo Antonia, John B. Levine, Anne Klibanski, Jill M. Goldstein, and Mohammed R. Milad, "Estradiol Modulates Medial Prefrontal Cortex and Amygdala Activity during Fear Extinction in Women and Female Rats," *Biological Psychiatry* 70, no. 10 (2011): 920–27.

5. J. K. Rieder, O. Kleshchova, and M. R. Weierich, "Estradiol, Stress Reactivity, and Daily Affective Experiences in Trauma-Exposed Women," *Psychological Trauma: Theory, Research, Practice, and Policy* 14, no. 5 (2002): 738–46, https://doi .org/10.1037/tra0001113.

6. Harriet A. Washington, *Medical Apartheid: The Dark History of Medical Experimentation on Black Americans from Colonial Times to the Present* (New York: Doubleday, 2006).

7. Benjamin Moseley, *A Treatise on Tropical Diseases, and on the Climate of the West Indies* (United Kingdom: T. Cadell, 1787).

8. Washington, *Medical Apartheid*, 2.

9. Donna L. Hoyert, "Maternal Mortality Rates in the United States, 2021," Center for Disease Control, March 16, 2023, https://doi.org/https://dx.doi .org/10.15620/cdc:124678.

10. Juanita J. China, Iman K. Martin, and Nicole Redmond, "Health Equity among Black Women in the United States," *Journal of Women's Health* 32, no. 2 (February 2021): 212–19, https://doi.org/10.1089/%2Fjwh.2020.8868.

11. John Hillard, "A Textbook Stereotyped How Racial Groups Respond to Pain. The Publisher Is Apologizing," *Boston Globe*, October 20, 2017, https://www .bostonglobe.com/arts/books/2017/10/20/publisher-apologizes-after-outcry -over-offensive-nursing-textbook/k6COKWl5ftuHsjooIxUK4K/story.html.

12. Jane Lawrence, "The Indian Health Service and the Sterilization of Native American Women," *The American Indian Quarterly* 24, no. 3 (2000): 400–419, https://doi.org/10.1353/aiq.2000.0008.

13. Judy Y. Chen, Allison L. Diamant, Marjorie Kagawa-Singer, Nadereh Pour, and Cheryl Wold, "Disaggregating Data on Asian and Pacific Islander Women to Assess Cancer Screening," *American Journal of Preventative Medicine* 27, no. 2 (2004): 139–45, https://doi.org/10.1016/j.amepre.2004.03.013.

14. Donna L. Hoyert, "Maternal Mortality Rates in the United States, 2021," *National Center for Health Statistics: Health Stats*, March 1, 2023, https://doi.org /10.15620/cdc:124678.

Chapter 2: Hagar

1. Karen Hunter and Pimpin' Ken, *Pimpology: The 48 Laws of the Game* (New York: Gallery Books, 2008), 66.

2. Hunter and Pimpin' Ken, *Pimpology*, 22.

Chapter 3: Leah and Dinah

1. "Serial Killers in the Philippines," Reddit, 2018, https://www.reddit.com/r /Philippines/comments/89o0ob/serial_killers_in_the_philippines.

2. Robin Dunbar, *Grooming, Gossip, and the Evolution of Language* (Cambridge, MA: Harvard University Press, 1996).

3. Alexander Fleisher and Zhenia Fleisher, "The Fragrance of Biblical Mandrake," *Economic Botany* 48 (1994): 243–51, https://doi.org/10.1007/BF02862323.

4. bell hooks, *The Will to Change: Men, Masculinity, and Love* (New York: Washington Square Press, 2005), 18.

5. Heidi Goettner-Abendroth, "Matriarchal Societies and Modern Matriarchal Studies," *The Legacy of Mothers: Matriarchies and the Gift Economy as Post-Capitalist Alternatives* (Toronto: Inanna Publications and Education, 2020), 106.

6. Robin Wall Kimmerer, *Braiding Sweetgrass* (Minneapolis: Milkweed Editions, 2020), 27.

7. Goettner-Abendroth, 105.

8. Goettner-Abendroth, 106.

9. Stephanie Buckhanon Crowder, *When Momma Speaks: The Bible and Motherhood from a Womanist Perspective* (Louisville, KY: Westminster John Knox Press, 2016).

Chapter 4: Potiphar's Wife

1. Tina Schermer Sellers, "How Spiritual Abuse Causes Complex Sexual Trauma," February 7, 2023, https://www.tinaschermersellers.com/post/how-spiritual-abuse-causes-symptoms-of-sexual-abuse.

2. Katelyn Beaty, "Joshua Harris and the Sexual Prosperity Gospel," Religion News Service, July 26, 2019, https://religionnews.com/2019/07/26/joshua-harris-and-the-sexual-prosperity-gospel/.

3. Centers for Disease Control, *Sexual Activity and Contraceptive Practices among Teenagers in the United States, 1988 and 1995*, May 2002, https://www.cdc.gov/nchs/data/series/sr_23/sr23_021.pdf, 12.

4. Anthony A. Mercadante and Prasanna Tadi, "Neuroanatomy, Gray Matter," National Library of Medicine, January 2022, https://www.ncbi.nlm.nih.gov/books/NBK553239.

5. Nandita Vijayakumar, Zdena Op de Macks, Elizabeth A. Shirtcliff, and Jennifer H. Pfeifer, "Puberty and the Human Brain: Insights to Adolescent Development," *Neuroscience and Biobehavioral Reviews* 92 (September 2018), https://www.ncbi.nlm.nih.gov/pmc/articles/PMC6234123/#R58.

6. Tina Schermer Sellers, "How the Purity Movement Causes Symptoms of Sexual Abuse," September 1, 2020, https://www.tinaschermersellers.com/post/how-the-purity-movement-causes-symptoms-of-sexual-abuse.

7. Sara Moslener, *Virgin Nation: Sexual Purity and American Adolescence* (New York: Oxford University Press, 2015), 3.

8. Tamura Lomax, *Jezebel Unhinged: Loosing the Black Female Body in Religion and Culture* (Durham, NC: Duke University Press, 2018), 25.

9. Centers for Disease Control and Prevention, *HIV Surveillance Report, 2019* (vol. 32), May 2021, http://www.cdc.gov/hiv/library/reports/hiv-surveillance.html.

10. Michelle Breunig, "Abstinence Only Sex Education Fails African American Youth," *Journal of Christian Nursing: A Quarterly Publication of Nurses Christian Fellowship* 34, no. 3 (July/September 2017): E41–E48, DOI: 10.1097/CNJ.0000000000000409.
11. Stephanie Kramer, "White Evangelicals More Likely Than Other Christians to Say People Should Prioritize Marriage, Procreation," Pew Research Center, December 16, 2021, https://www.pewresearch.org/fact-tank/2021/12/16/white-evangelicals-more-likely-than-other-christians-to-say-people-should-prioritize-marriage-procreation.
12. David Masci and Claire Gecewicz, "Share of Married Adults Varies Widely across U.S. Religious Groups," Pew Research Center, March 19, 2018, https://www.pewresearch.org/fact-tank/2018/03/19/share-of-married-adults-varies-widely-across-u-s-religious-groups.
13. Tiffany Bluhm, *Prey Tell: Why We Silence Women Who Tell the Truth and How Everyone Can Speak Up* (Grand Rapids, MI: Brazos Press, 2021), 113.

Chapter 5: Rahab

1. Garci Rodriguez de Montalvo, *Las Sergas de Esplandián*, trans. Robert S. Rudder (Claremont, CA: Svenson Publishers, 2019), 333.
2. Wil Gafney, "Who Are You Calling a Whore?" October 19, 2014, https://www.wilgafney.com/2014/10/19/who-are-you-calling-a-whore.
3. Miriame Kaba, *We Do This 'Til We Free Us* (Chicago: Haymarket Books, 2021), 37.
4. Kaba, *We Do This*, 142.
5. Patrisse Cullors, *An Abolitionist's Handbook* (New York: St. Martin's Press, 2021), 187.
6. Lisa Sharon Harper, Twitter message, February 26, 2019, https://twitter.com/lisasharper/status/1100521159320367105?ref_src=twsrc%5Etfw%7Ctwcamp%5Emoment%7Ctwgr%5EeyJ0ZndfdHdlZXRfZWRpdF9iYWNrZW5kIjp7Im J1Y2tldCI6Im9mZiIsInZlcnNpb24iOm51bGx9LCJ0ZndfcmVmc3JjX3Nlc3N pb24iOnsiYnVja2V0Ijoib2ZmIiwidmVyc2lvbiI6bnVsbH0sI.
7. Inger Burnett-Zeigler, *Nobody Knows the Trouble I've Seen: Exploring the Emotional Lives of Black Women* (New York: HarperCollins, 2021), 52.
8. Allyson Tintiango-Cubales and R. Edward Curammeng, "Pedagogies of Resistance: Filipina/o Gestures of Rebellion in American Schooling," in *Education at War*, ed. Arshad Imtiaz Ali and Tracy Lachica Buenavista (New York: Fordham University Press, 2018), 236.

Chapter 6: Jael

1. Lama Rod Owens, *Love and Rage: The Path of Liberation through Anger* (Berkeley, CA: North Atlantic Books, 2020), 228.
2. George M. Johnson, *All Boys Aren't Blue: A Memoir-Manifesto* (New York: Farrar, Straus and Giroux, 2020), 1.
3. United Nations Office on Genocide Prevention and the Responsibility to Protect, "Sexual Violence: A Tool of War," Outreach Program on the Rwanda Genocide and the United Nations, United Nations, March 1, 2014, https://